Tales of a Country Girl

"Growing up on a Two Mule Farm"

Lois Wehunt Stewart

Tales of a Country Girl

"Growing up on a Two Mule Farm"

Lois Wehunt Stewart

Published By:
Brentwood Christian Press
4000 Beallwood Avenue
Columbus, Georgia 31904

In Cooperation With
Marble Valley Friends, Inc.
Post Office Box 2
Tate, Georgia 30177
"Remembering the Past and Looking to the Future"

Dedication

To my husband Bob who loves me and my "country girl" ways and helped make the book come together. To my children, Robert, Jenny and Mike for encouraging me to put my stories in writing. To Robert, who spent valuable time formatting these writings into book form.

Foreword

A look back is not to yearn for the good old days but to recognize that some of the old ways were good and to hope that some of the goodness can be recaptured.

Contents

GROWING UP ON
A TWO MULE FARM

It was the year 1927, Christmas Eve, to be exact, in the county of Cherokee, in the hills of north Georgia. However, I do not remember it. You see, that was the day I was born.

I was the sixth girl born to Luther and Everet Wehunt. Two boys were sandwiched smack dab in the middle of the girls. Three more boys would be born later, to make a large family of eleven children altogether.

My first faint remembrances were of living in a house called the Faulkner place that had a private family cemetery surrounded by an iron fence. I presume members of the Faulkner family were buried there. My first three years were spent here. During this time my grandfather Wehunt lived with us. In my childish fancy I remember my grandfather as resembling Santa Claus because of his full white beard.

The other memory I have of that place concerns a hen and her biddies. Chickens had free run of the yard in those days. In this particular incident, a hen was scratching in the yard to find insects for the chicks. I decided to help her out by turning over a large rock. You could always find a lot of insects under a country rock. Unfortunately the biddies were too close and several of the chicks were killed by the rock as it turned over. To make matters worse, in my panic I turned the rock back over crushing more of the chicks. I recall crying with regret. I don't remember the outcome of this my first tragedy. Whether I was punished or not, it is forever etched in my memory.

The community was called Frogtown, presumably because it was near a river and there were a lot of frogs croaking. I must have been about four when we moved here. Another name for the community was "Steal Easy." Perhaps at one time it had been easy to steal things there. Or maybe it was spelled "Still Easy" from being an easy place to build a whiskey still and make "moonshine." We never knew the reason for the name.

Only a few memories stand out about our second house. I remember a wide porch around at least two sides of the house where we children romped and played, especially on rainy days. One outstanding memory is Mama's fear of storms. Mama had a near phobia over severe weather. We were never allowed to play on the porch if there was any hint of thunder or lighting. Even a distant rumble of thunder found her going from one window to another looking at the clouds to see whether they were coming closer or gathering over head. She would not let us touch any metal. I distinctly remember her forbidding us to cut paper dolls from the Sears Catalog with metal scissors. She made us stay toward the middle of the room, away from the windows. Today's instruction from the National Weather Service has some of the same directions. Modern times for you!

Although Mama was terrified of storms, I never heard her tell of a bad or tragic experience with tornadoes or thunderstorms. From her actions, I deducted that she must have had one.

There was a storm cellar on this property in Frogtown. It was down near the barn, a few yards from the house. Actually it was a cave-like room dug out in the side of a high bank. Dug out benches lined the sides of the cellar. I don't remember whether the roof was shored up with some kind of timbers. It must have been, but from outside the top was only earth. What is clear in my memory is being awakened in the middle of the night, and hurried to the cellar when a storm occurred. Quilts were carried to sit on, or for the children to lie on. With the door closed it was completely dark. We had a kerosene lantern, but did not keep it lit after entering because of the cost and the fumes. Dad would peek out to see whether it was all right to return to the house.

There was a story told to me by my sister Clora, which I had never heard before I started writing the above account. Mama did have traumatic experiences with storms. When she was a little girl one of their cows had a calf that Mama called hers. The cow and calf were in a lot by the barn when a storm came up. When Mama and her brother went to put them in the shelter, she climbed upon the fence. Lightening struck, killing the calf and knocking Mama to the ground." Now I understand that Mama's fear of stormy weather was founded on a bad experience.

My sister told me of other times when storms did damage to the Faulkner house. The end of the shop building was blown out twice. Once Dad and Herb were in the shop. They came running to the house, Dad still holding the shop tool he had been working with. Another time lightning struck a tree next to the house shattering windows and knocking Grandpa to his knees. Mama had good reason to fear stormy weather.

The next house that we lived in did not have a storm cellar, so Dad put up lightning rods, which helped Mama feel safer.

DINNER FOR THE PRISONERS

During the years we lived in Frogtown, convicts from the jail worked on the roads in our area. They wore striped clothes, and those who were considered dangerous or likely to escape wore heavy chains with iron balls attached to their ankles. I had never seen a black person before. A few of the convicts were black. People called them niggers but it was not used in a derogatory manner where we lived. It was descriptive, as was the word Spanish or French or Indian. We children were not afraid of the prisoners. We played around near where they were working and talked with them.

The roads must have been pretty bad, and the prisoners must have worked long and hard getting them in good condition. To show appreciation to them, when they had finished, the community had a big dinner for them on the picnic tables in the churchyard. People brought fried chicken, vegetables, cakes and pies. It was a fun time for the whole crowd. Perhaps it influenced the prisoners to live a better life.

9

LEARNING IN A ONE ROOM SCHOOL

My first school was in Frogtown. Small neighborhood schools were customary. The building was one room with seven grades plus primer. One teacher taught all. What was called primer then was a substitute for kindergarten of today. The difference was that we had a "reader" and learned to read. We were also disciplined the same as older students, expected to behave and be quiet, and took no naps. We learned a lot from listening to the older children recite. The whole seven grades were no more than one room of thirty or so students.

The children of family farmers were scattered over the countryside and walked to school. We lived only about a half-mile away so it was a short walk for us. Most of the children lived close enough to run home for lunch.

The schoolroom was heated in winter with a wood burning potbelly stove. On very cold days we huddled around it to keep warm. Only one side of us was warm at one time - the side toward the stove. Parents cut and furnished the wood. Older children were responsible for bringing it in and keeping the fire going.

Windows were open in summer to catch any cool breeze. The noises outside could be quite distracting to young children who would rather be outside playing than studying, especially in the springtime. Naturally recess was a favorite time.

Water was dipped from a bubbling spring with a gourd into a galvanized bucket. The bucket was filled and brought from the spring to the schoolroom each day by one of the older children. All children drank from the same gourd. No one thought about catching germs or infections drinking from the same gourd in those days. After all we visited in each other's home and drank the same way.

Paddling was an approved way of punishment for children who misbehaved at school in days of yore. I know this because I received a paddling in the primer grade here. It was summer session and all the children came to school barefoot. My big toe was sore, for what reason I don't recall - a bee sting, a cut from glass or sharp stick? It was tied up with a rag, which must have been clean when applied but didn't stay clean long. This was before Band-Aids.

Here is what happened that resulted in my paddling. Some of the others and I were playing near the spring which was the source of our drinking water. We were probably wading in the water below the spring when one dared me to stick my sore toe in the spring. Being a very precocious child I did just that. Immediately the other child ran and told the teacher. The paddling probably did not hurt so much as my hurt pride, because I do not recall what kind of paddle she used. To this day at reunions my siblings still tease me about sticking my sore toe in the spring.

THE DEPRESSION

When Wall Street crashed, I was two years old. The days of the depression that followed really made little difference to poor farm families. We didn't know we were poor. Neighbors and people we knew were living the same way. There was no TV to show us "The Lifestyles of the Rich and Famous."

Family farms were self-sustaining to a degree. Practically all of the food consumed was grown and processed at home. Vegetables from the garden were canned or dried. Potatoes, sweet and white, were stored in the storm cellar with straw around them. If there was no storm cellar, a pit was dug and lined with straw. The site was carefully selected for good drainage so that no rainwater collected inside.

Meats consisting of pork and poultry were raised on all farms. Chicken dumplings were a favorite food, but sometimes we had rabbit or squirrel dumplings if Dad and my brothers were lucky hunting.

Eggs were usually plentiful, as were milk and butter. Cows were kept only for milk, never for slaughter, at least not with families I knew, so we ate no beef.

Corn was raised for cornmeal and feed for the animals. Sorghum cane was grown for syrup and for sweetener. Honey from beehives provided another source of sweetening.

11

Most farms had a grape vine and apple tree for fruit and jelly. Wild blackberries, dewberries and huckleberries (a wild type of blueberry) were picked for jellies, jams and pies.

BRAMBLE SCRAMBLE FOR BLACKBERRIES

Most of the blackberries were found at the edge of the field but it was necessary sometimes to scramble into the brambles to find the biggest juiciest ones. Though we were well prepared, berry picking was both an adventure and a punishment. They were so good, but oh those briars and chiggers! First we dressed in the heaviest long sleeve shirt and overalls on some of the hottest days of the year. This gave some protection against briars. We rubbed kerosene on our ankles and wrists to keep the chiggers off. It smelled awful and burned somewhat, but it really worked. We could not avoid the berry stains on our fingers that remained for days. If the weather had been good we could pick gallons and many times we had enough to trade at the store. The family who owned the store was always happy to get them because they were a popular item with town people who would stop and buy them.

Processing the berries, especially dewberries and blackberries, took a good part of the day. First the berries were heated just enough to free the juice. Next they were placed in a clean white flour sack and kneaded, squeezed and twisted to get every drop of juice possible. The correct amount of sugar was added and the mix brought to a boil on the hot stove. Careful watching was required. To be of the right consistency the jelly should hang from the spoon in two globs. The jelly shouldn't be too thin or thick. It was necessary to boil the jars, rubber rings and tops to sterilize them. Jelly was poured into the jars and sealed while very hot, being careful not to burn one's self. Jelly was sometimes sealed with melted paraffin.

There is no comparison of the real flavor of berry jams and jellies made in those days with the bland taste of today's cultivated berries. The wild flavor is missing. The taste of mass-produced jellies and jams can't hold a candle to those homemade of yore. Never mind all the briar scratches, the chiggers, stains and the cooking and stirring over the hot wood burning stove. Homemade jelly on hot homemade biscuits at breakfast was worth it.

SUN-DRIED APPLES

If you've never eaten sun-dried apples you've missed a treat. Any other way to dry them just doesn't produce the same flavor. A table was made with sawhorses and planks and placed in the sun. The peeled sliced apples were spread in one layer on a sheet of cloth on the table. The drying process took more than one day, as I remember bringing them in at night. The children were assigned turns to keep the flies off. A "Fly Minder" was made with a long stick, about a fourth inch in diameter. It was inserted in the fold of a sheet of newspaper. Then the paper was sewn with needle and thread near the stick close enough to hold it on the stick. The paper then was cut into strips up to the thread. This made an excellent "Fly-Minder." It reached across the table and was waved constantly. When the apples were golden brown and dried sufficiently they were packed in glass jars or in small cloth bags. To store them the bags were hung in a dry place.

To use the apples we needed to soak them in water for some time. Mama made a yummy stacked cake with the dried apple filling in between. It didn't look like a cake, but more like a stack of large pancakes. I remember it as being scrumptious. I wish I knew the recipe but Mama usually did not cook from a recipe. She just used a pinch of this and that, and a dollop of lard or butter, and handfuls of flour.

We were such a big family she often made deep-dish cobbler in the dishpan, which was made of enameled metal. It probably held a gallon at least. Care had to be taken with grape cobbler to pick out the seeds as we ate. Huckleberry, blackberry, peach, apple or grape cobbler was delicious sweetened with either homemade sorghum or honey. The crust was made with homemade butter and it almost melted in your mouth.

13

SCRATCHING OUT A LIVING

Scratching out a living was not easy on the farm but we knew no other life style and were happy and satisfied for the most part.

Let's take a look at survival on a family farm with poor soil and little else. The cash crop was cotton. Enough was raised to pay for things we could not produce, or barter for. Some of these were medicines, kerosene for the lamps, items to repair harness for the mules and wagon and nails.

Shoes were one item of clothing we couldn't make at home. Dad had an iron "shoe-last" that shoes were placed on for repair. He often resoled our shoes with scraps of leather taken from old shoes that could no longer be repaired. They were made to last as long as possible.

Many things were fertilized with good old manure, (mule, cow, and chicken) which was worked into the soil. Dad needed to buy fertilizer for the corn and cotton since the existence of the farm depended upon corn, to make our bread and feed for the animals. Cotton was our cash crop and needed a good start with fertilizer also.

It was a great day for us if Dad permitted one of us to go to the cotton gin with him. The wagonload of cotton was driven underneath a large vacuum pipe. From there it was sucked up and carried through the carding process that removed the seeds. Then it was compressed into a huge bale. Most of the time it was sold at the gin, but occasionally Dad brought the bale home probably thinking the price might go up later. The seeds retrieved from the ginning process were ground into cottonseed meal and stored in "tow" sacks in the barn for food for the cows. A tow sack is the country name for a burlap bag.

In summer plants and grass were plentiful, so the cows and mules got much of their food grazing in the pasture. This was supplemented with dried corn on the cob for the mules and hogs. The mules also got fodder. Fodder was bundles of corn leaves, which were stripped off the stalk by hand carefully because the edge of the leaves were sharp and could cut our hands if they were not callused. These leaves were tied into bundles with another corn leaf or two. There was an art to getting the right amount and tying it neatly such a way that it would not come apart with wear. This was done after the corn was harvested we went along the rows stripping and tying fodder. It was tossed onto the wagon, as the wagon was driven down the rows. One person stood on the wagon placing the bundles so they wouldn't fall off on the way to the barn. When they arrived at the barn, one person stood on the wagon and tossed one bundle at a time to another person up in the barn (hay) loft. This took skill and an accurate aim because the opening in the loft was only about three feet by three feet.

In addition to the corn, hogs were fed "slop." This was a mixture of table scraps, vegetable hulls and peels, and fruit peels. Those hogs didn't know what healthy food they were eating! Today we are urged to eat the peel of potatoes and fruit, the hulls with the peas, and the bran that we sifted from the corn and grains. There was no need for garbage pick-up in those days. The hogs took care of that problem.

Neither was there need for recycling programs. Newspapers and catalogs were used to line the kitchen pie safe, stop up cracks in the wall, start fires in the fireplace, in the wood burning cook stove, and under the wash pot on wash days. Also important, newspaper or the Sears catalogs were used for toilet tissue in the outhouse.

I don't remember having many things in tin cans, perhaps a can of pineapple once or twice a year. Pineapple sandwiches at the "May Meeting" were a real treat. Any tin cans, boxes and brush from the yard were tossed into a deep gully nearby, which we were anxious to fill.

BAREFOOT AMUSEMENTS

Most kids went barefoot in the summer, except for our "Sunday Go to Meeting Shoes" that we wore to "meeting," our name for church. Sometimes it was called "preaching." For example, some one might ask, "Are you going to preaching today?"

Long before it was warm enough in the spring we begged Mama to go barefoot. We loved the feel of the porcelain-smooth red clay of the dirt road just after the "cattie-pillers," (our name for the county road scrapers) had been by.

The rain on the dry soil produced a wonderful earthy odor. It was quite enticing to young adventurers. We found endless amusement in the mud after a good rain. We loved making a "squishy hole." We would find a soft spot and slowly walk our feet up and down in the same place to see who could make the deepest "squishy." It really felt good and cool in the hot summer. We could often get up to our knees in mud.

Making frog houses was another mud game. We made frog houses by packing mud over the front part of our feet. Then we carefully pulled our feet out so as not to collapse the house. You can bet Mama frowned on our entering the house without washing our feet after these shenanigans.

There were also perils to going barefoot. Stepping on a big bumblebee or wasp was sure to produce a sting and swollen foot. To ease the pain we applied a mixture of baking soda and vinegar. It still works today.

Running through the yard helter-skelter we could catch a "red nose" briar vine between our toes. The vine was long with many sharp thorns, and before we could stop it would cause such pain we felt as if our toe was almost sawed off. Of course, we stepped on other briars and splinters but the "red nose" was the worst. Still the fun of being barefoot out weighed the accidents.

PUNISHMENT - THE HICKORY SWITCH

We tried to avoid punishment at all costs and were pretty successful. Mama and Dad were strict and we knew and kept within the boundaries they had set for us. Nevertheless we sometimes forgot and had to face the music. We were more threatened than punished. Mama would say, "If you don't behave I'll get a switch and stripe your legs." That was usually all we needed.

16

Dad used a straight razor, keeping it sharp with a leather strop. He often threatened to take the razor strop to us when we misbehaved. I don't remember his ever carrying out the threat. His thunder and lightning lectures had us sadly ruing our wicked ways. We had much rather face Mama's hickory switch than Dad's barrage of words.

The switching I most remember from Mama was administered for luring my brother Ken out in the wet damp mud and rain. Although he was quite as eager as I to get out and play, I was older and should be more responsible. Ken had very bad spells with asthma during which he had trouble breathing. It was thought that playing in the rain and dampness brought on his attacks. There were several instances when Mama striped my legs blaming me for his being in the rain even though he was not sick at the time. Of course we know now the dampness has nothing to do with asthma.

CLOTHING: HAND-ME DOWNS AND MAKE DO

"Store-bought" clothes were few. Shoes were one of those few. In the winter all the children wore high top lace up shoes. We thought they were ugly but they were durable and warm for winter wear. Now in the 90's this is the latest fashion, all the rage among young people through college age. Those that are popular now are the very heavy ones like the men wore. I still think they are ugly. We called them clodhoppers.

With the high top shoes, girls wore long brown cotton stockings held up by a piece of elastic above the knee. Our elastic leg bloomers came down over the tops of the stockings but were hidden by our longer dresses. Most of the elastic we used was a strip of rubber cut from an old inner tube that could no longer be patched for use in a car.

Shoes were sometimes purchased from the country store with bartered goods. Other times they were ordered from the Sears Roebuck catalog. The way we ordered the right size shoes was to step on a piece of paper and draw our foot size to send to Sears

Roebuck to order shoes. We had one pair of everyday shoes for school and one pair of slippers for Sunday. Shoes as well as other clothing were handed down from older children who had outgrown them to younger ones. Overalls for the boys and heavy coats were ordered when none was available as hand downs. More often they were bought from the country store in exchange for goods.

A new dress was a real treat. Material for dresses was ordered from Sears, perhaps twice a year. The price I remember so well was nine cents a yard for cotton goods. I tried very hard to save enough money I earned to buy cloth for a dress. It was very exciting for us to watch for the mailman, anticipating the delivery of a package.

To send the order one of us had to wait beside the mailbox for the mailman with the money and order blank filled out to buy a money order. We had a particularly gruff mailman of whom we were a bit scared. If we were not right there waiting he would pass on by and not stop. Then we had to wait another day to send the order. We called our mailman "Old Page." Page was his last name. I never knew his first name.

ADVENTURES AT THE COUNTRY STORE

The country store was a fascinating experience. It had just about everything we could imagine and much more than we could afford. There we didn't need money to buy things, no indeed! The name of the store where we traded was Sartors and was owned by Mr. and Mrs. Sartor. It was about two or three miles away from our home over a dusty dirt road. The most common way to get there was by foot. However if something heavy was needed such as fertilizer Dad took the wagon.

I remember my sister, Oveda, and I walking the three miles to the store. She carried the bucket of eggs and I had a chicken in each hand. She was older and the eggs would be safer in her care, besides she was scared of the chickens. The chickens were squawking because we tied their feet together and carried them upside down by their feet. Sometimes they got away but they couldn't run far into the woods with their feet tied and we could catch them easily. The event would make a great comedy sketch on a country show today and seems quite amusing to recall.

Many times we had extra butter to trade and sometimes berries or nuts or other farm products.

The coffee we traded for was Luzianne and was part chicory. To make coffee, we boiled it in an old blue enamel pot. The grounds settled to the bottom and we were careful not to shake them up when pouring it. Whoever got the last cupful usually drank carefully because it contained grounds. When I was small and begged for coffee Mama would pour a little into my glass of milk. To this day I like my coffee quite white with milk or creamer.

We used a large quantity of flour for biscuits, gravy, cakes and coating food for frying. It was one of the items we traded for. Flour came in printed floral and plaid sacks, but sometimes in plain white. These were valuable items for our household. Many items of clothing were made of flour sacks.

My older sister Thenia was our family seamstress. I don't know how she happened to assume this responsibility. She seemed to have a natural talent though. The old foot- pedal Singer sewing machine responded magically to her touch. She didn't need a pattern. She could look at a picture in the catalog and make a dress fashioned after it. We thought the dresses she made of material we ordered from Sears were perfect. She could do smocking, embroidery, and other fancy needlework. She made everyday dresses and shirts and pillowcases from the colored flour sacks. She made dishtowels and the girls' underwear, "bloomers," from the white ones.

A FAMILY OF TEN IN A FOUR-ROOM HOUSE

By the time I was seven, about 1935, we moved to Pickens County. It was here that I lived until I went away to college. Most of my childhood memories occurred here. I was old enough to assume duties and work in the fields.

Here is how we came to move to this house. My sister Clora, at age 21, had married Hallman Fouts in 1934. Clora's husband was only to live 16 months after they were married. Meanwhile Dad acquired from them enough property for a family farm.

The family pronounces her name Clorie. Somehow names ending with "a" tended to become "ie," or "e" in pronunciation in our neck of the woods. My oldest sister named Lenora became Le-nore, accent on the first syllable, and Thenia was Thenie.

In most large families children are usually born not more than a year apart, but in ours there was at least two years, and more often three years or more between each child. Dad named most all the children in his big family, of which he was very proud. Some names he took from the Bible and some from Mama's folks and his. He received some criticism for naming the youngest boy Sherman, but it was not the Yankee general for whom he was named but some ancestor.

Let's continue with the story of the house. The house on the property Dad bought was made of wood. It was painted white on the outside and had four rooms with a stone fireplace in one room and a wide porch across the front. The house had a wooden plank ceiling but no insulation. The walls were made of rough unpainted planks of one thickness. The roof was made of tin. Later Dad would add two more rooms, which were used for a kitchen and a bedroom. He also built a back porch.

We moved into the four rooms before my two younger brothers were born, so there were five girls, three boys and Dad and Mama. The living room fireplace provided the only heat in the house except for the kitchen stove. The living room or "front room" as it was commonly called was also Mama and Dad's bedroom. The babies were kept in that room while little, too. Besides the iron bed it was furnished with ladder-back cane bottomed chairs. These could be moved close to the fireplace in cold weather and also moved to the kitchen table for meals.

A very old fashioned table sat next to one wall. It was covered with a crocheted cloth on which sat the kerosene lamp and the family Bible. A collection of small vases and trinkets sat on the bottom shelf of the table. Later a bookcase next to the fireplace held my brother's collection of Zane Grey books.

The mantle over the fireplace had a lovely old wind up clock that struck the hour and half-hour. One of the first sounds of the morning was Dad winding the clock and setting it; this was a morning ritual. Next he would start a fire in the kitchen stove and start heating water for coffee. In winter Dad would build a fire in the fireplace. Using the coals of the smoldering backlog he had covered with ashes the night before to keep it live, made the fire easy to start.

Before Dad built the other rooms the kitchen was also the dining room. On one side were the wood burning stove and a wood box. In the middle was the home made table long enough to seat the whole family. The table was covered with a colorful oilcloth that was easy to clean. The pie safe, an antique treasure today, sat next to a wall and contained the dishes and whatever food was leftover. There was no electricity, no refrigerator or icebox. Sugar, spices and other goods were stored in the pie safe. In summer when ants were invasive we put a saucer filled with water under each leg to keep ants out. It was effective because ants cannot swim.

A large black three-legged cast iron pot with a sturdy wire handle sat on the stove. Peas, beans and other vegetables were cooked in it. The eye could be removed from the stove and the pot set directly over the fire. The black iron water kettle usually sat directly over the fire also. Consequently the bottoms of both was quite sooty with smoke. Care had to be taken so it didn't smear on other things. A big iron frying pan was used to cook many things. Fried okra, potatoes, corn, and chicken were some foods cooked in it. An aluminum double boiler, cake pans and pans for corn bread and biscuits completed the cookware.

We used a hodge-podge of mismatched dishes, forks, knives and spoons. Sometimes a plate would come inside a box of laundry detergent creating a desire to buy more to complete the set. Other products had promotions offering a free plate or bowl. Oatmeal boxes always contained a cup, saucer or cereal bowl. These were made of Depression glass and are now highly collectable.

Next to the wall sat the flour and meal bin. This was a wooden piece counter high. It was divided into two compartments. One side held flour, the flour sifter and the rolling pin. The other side held cornmeal and the meal sifter. The top made a nice work counter.

The front bedroom had two double beds and an old dresser with a mirror. When we acquired the pump organ it found a home in one corner of this room. The two older sisters slept in one bed and we three young girls in the other. There were always arguments over who would sleep in the middle, an undesirable position. As the youngest, I usually lost out. There were shelves next to the wall where we kept our few clothes A curtain hung on a string in front to hide it.

The bedrooms were unheated and were shivery cold in winter. We often put a rock near the fireplace to warm, wrapped it in a cloth, and placed it in the foot of our bed to warm our feet. We slept under several quilts that were warm but quite heavy. By morning the rock was cold but body heat had warmed the bed.

The boys, Herschel, Herbert, Kenneth, and Sam slept in the other bedroom. Herbert would marry and move away before my youngest brother was born. His oldest child would be about the same age as my youngest brother.

Sounds carried throughout the house since the plank walls were not insulated. Dad's snoring could be heard throughout the house. The sound tended to be comforting to me if I waked from a bad dream. I knew that if Dad was there I was safe. That's probably why my husband's snoring never bothered me.

It seems almost impossible that we could have overnight company in such crowded quarters. We did, and it was very exciting. Distances seemed much farther in the slow pace of wagon travel or later T-Model cars. So when kin came to visit they stayed a while. It was usually summer time when our cousins came to visit. We kids all slept on a pallet on the floor and allowed the grown up guests to use the beds. Spreading several homemade quilts on the floor made "pallets." Kids today call this kind of visit a slumber party. We slumbered about as much then as today's kids do. We knew though, that we had to keep quiet so the grown ups could sleep.

On rare occasions we would have a friend to "stay all night." Most of our friends lived so close they could easily go home at night and that is what their parents preferred. Later when we made friends in high school they could ride the school bus home with us to spend the night.

During revival meetings the neighbors took turns "sleeping" the visiting preacher. We always enjoyed the preachers. Preachers must be born comedians because they had, and still do, pockets full of funny stories that delighted us. Revivals were always in the summer during laying by time and the weather was warm enough to make pallets on the porch, which was a treat. The plaintive call of the whippoorwill, owls and other night sounds lulled us into a peaceful sleep.

The back porch served many purposes especially during summer. There was a long shelf along one side of the porch. It held the bucket of drinking water with an aluminum dipper. On the shelf was also an enamel washbasin along with a bar of Lifebuoy soap for washing hands. Towels hung on a heavy string above the shelf.

Chairs were brought out to sit in while preparing foods to cook, or can, shelling peas or snapping beans. If a neighbor happened by she might sit and visit while the vegetables were being prepared. The vegetables were carried to the spring to wash rather than bring up extra water.

The back porch was also a place to take off muddy shoes or shoes that were kept solely for work where they were soiled with manure. If it had been raining wet coats were hung on the porch to dry before entering the house. The back porch was both an entry and a workplace.

The use of the front porch was more for relaxing and entertaining company. It had a three-person swing. Chairs were often moved there from inside and visitors were entertained on the porch. Sometimes we would sit there after dark and sing. As children we often sat on the edge of the porch floor with our feet dangling off. It was restful especially after a hard day at work in the fields. We enjoyed sitting and listening to the pleasant song of the Whippoorwill. We listened to crickets and frogs and sometime caught "lightning bugs" (fireflies). They had a very unpleasant odor especially when crushed so we held them very tenderly. We put them in a jar and put holes for air in the top with a nail. This was a child's homemade flashlight. We released them before going to bed. If we forgot we found them all dead next morning and felt very sad.

Although children loved the front porch swing, it had a special place in the hearts of young gals and guys. The front porch swing was often the place where sweethearts sat when a fellow came calling on Sunday afternoon or evening. Courting couples were given priority on those occasions. Many lifetime matches were made in the front porch swing. Couples who were seeing each other regularly were said to be "sparking." My brother sparked his wife doubly because her last name was Sparks.

The doors of the house had a knob and an old fashioned lock that could be opened with a common skeleton key. I don't remember a key because the door was never locked. Even when we walked up the hill to church, I remember being the first one home and simply opening the door. In the summer the wooden doors were left open for ventilation and the screen door was latched with a small insignificant fastener. This was more to keep prowling animal out than people. People were more honest in those days. Also, we were remotely located and had little to attract thieves.

One important feature of the house was lightning rods, which Dad put up to please Mama because there was no storm shelter here. They were installed on top of the house at each end of the roof and were grounded with wires. If lightning struck it would hit the rods, travel down the wires to the ground causing no damage or danger to the house and it's occupants.

Another interesting feature of the house was the tin roof. If you've never heard the sound of rain on a tin roof you've missed something. A soft rain could lull you to sleep or a hard rain could seem threatening. Depending on your mood the sound was sometimes soothing, sometimes ominous, but unforgettable.

The house had no underpinning and was open underneath. I remember crawling under the house to play but do not remember what we played. Perhaps we hid during hide and seek games. The ground was always dry and sandy under the house. We could draw pictures in the sand with a stick, and find "doodlebug homes." Doodlebugs were tiny burrowing insects. They made a depression in the sand by working sand around to resemble an empty cone. Smaller insects daring to land in the depression could not get out of the small bank of sand. The Doodlebug came out of hiding under the sand and had his dinner. We could entice him out by lightly touching a twig to the sand. Sometimes we did so for hours on end.

MUSIC - FUN FOR ALL

Dad loved music and always had some kind of instrument around. At various times, or sometimes together, he had a mandolin, banjo, guitar, and Jew's harp. He was never very fluent on any instrument, playing only simple chords, but his interest instilled a love of music in all of us. One song I remember him playing and singing was; "The bear went over the mountain," (sing this line three times)" To see what he could see." "The other side of the mountain," (sing three times) "Was all that he could see."

Another was, "The sheep and billy goat a'going to the pasture. The sheep said, 'Goat can't you go a little faster?' The sheep fell down and broke his shin. Oh, my goodness how the goat did grin." Dad had a sense of humor and liked a funny song as well as a good joke.

It was very exciting when we acquired a pump organ. Three of us girls learned to play by ear. Many times the family would gather round and sing the old time gospel songs. Later when I took piano lessons in high school I practiced on it even though the action was not the same.

25

MAMA AND HER MUSIC

Mama liked music and sang too. Most of the family said Mama couldn't "carry a tune in a bucket." She could, but only one. Every thing she sang was to the same tune. I still begged her to sing to me as she made biscuits or worked in the kitchen. I loved to hear her sing the old story-telling ballads like *Barbara Allen*, *The Ballad of Little Mary Fagin and Leo Frank*, *Old 97* (a train wreck song), *Casey Jones*, *Floyd Collins* (who died exploring a cave, after many days of rescue attempts) and others. Most newsworthy events had songs composed to tell the story.

Mama resembled the typical pioneer woman. Her long brown hair was pulled away from her face and wound in a bun at the back of her head. Her high cheekbones and coloring suggested Indian ancestry. She wore a long dress with a large apron. In my minds eye I can still see her gathering up the corners of her apron as a substitute for a basket, and filling it with beans or other garden goodies. It was her favorite way to carry things.

I would describe Mama as somewhat shy. Instead of talking she listened to others. It was just as well. With such a large family she probably had trouble getting in a word edgewise! She was short and plump around the middle. She was easygoing and usually very patient. Having so many babies had played havoc with her figure. Although her life was hard she never complained.

Mama's favorite hymn type song was, *Life is Like a Mountain Railroad*. I'd like to record the words here, because it says something about her character and her faith.

Life is like a mountain railroad,
With an engineer that's brave.
We must make the run successful
From the cradle to the grave.
Watch the curves, the hills, the tunnels
Never falter, never fail
Keep your hand upon the throttle
And your eye upon the rail.

Chorus
Blessed Savior, thou wilt guide us
'Til we reach that blissful shore.
Where the angels wait to join us
In thy praise forever more.

My sister Clora was left a record player by her first husband. It was a piece of furniture in itself, cased in a lovely wood cabinet. It played cylinder type records that were shaped like a water glass with no bottom. The children were not allowed to play it because the head with the needle had to be placed carefully on the record or it would be scratched and damaged beyond repair. The records broke or cracked easily. The player was wound by turning a crank-like handle and care was taken not to wind it tight enough to break the spring. We were delighted when grown ups played it for us. There were quite a number of records.

ALL DAY SINGINGS

Many of the small churches that dotted the north Georgia countryside held "all day singings with dinner on the ground" each year. Perhaps at sometime dinner was served as a picnic on the ground but not when I was growing up. Dinner was served on rough homemade picnic tables covered with embroidered tablecloths. Some of the best fried chicken, vegetables and coconut cake ever baked was consumed at these gatherings.

Gospel quartets and groups from all around came, both to perform and to sing together for the love of singing. It was at these events that new songs were learned, and new songbooks were available. If a special group was not performing everyone was welcome to sing. The loudest was not always the best and most pleasant voice to listen to, but everyone had a good time. It was always a social event. Usually whole families attended and you had a chance to visit with neighbors and perhaps make new friends. Young girls hoped the fellow they liked would talk to them or at least send a smile their way.

COUNTY SINGING CONVENTIONS - A GREAT HOLIDAY

The highlight of the year was The County Singing Convention held at the courthouse in Jasper, the county seat of Pickens County. It was like a holiday and lasted from early until late. We were lucky if we were able to go, because of transportation. We lived at least ten miles away, too far to walk. It was not practical to drive the wagon so far as there was no provision for mules. Neighbors who had a car sometimes pooled rides.

Groups from all over the state and some from other nearby states came. Many times well-known quartets attended. There were people who sang the shape notes and could sing notes rather than words to the songs. I never learned this and it sounded quite strange. Workshops were held where people could learn to become song leaders.

When we got tired of sitting and listening, (although you could hear the music from the streets), we would walk down the street. If we were lucky enough to have a nickel tied in our hanky, (which is how we girls most often carried our coin, or coins), we would get an ice cream cone, a Popsicle, or a Nugrape Soda. This was really a treat because we had no refrigeration at home and ice cream was very rare for us.

Of course there was gospel hymn singing at regular church services. There was no group of singers called the choir. The singers would gather round the old pump organ, (later on a piano was used) at the front of the church. They sang several hymns before the preacher began his sermon. I don't remember the congregation joining in the singing as in churches today. Perhaps all the people who felt they could sing joined the singers around the piano or the pump organ.

YOUNG PEOPLE, JAM SESSIONS AND ROMANCE

Most people in the country could sing to some degree. Occasionally we teenagers (and soon to be teenagers) got together on Saturday night to sing "Grand Ole Opry" type songs. We walked to someone's home, usually the Lawsons because Jim and Blanche, who were about our age, had guitars and could play very well. Others brought harmonicas or banjos. There were always several people who could "pick and make music" in the neighborhood. We all knew the words to many songs. This was often our Saturday evening entertainment.

There were no concerts in our area. Transportation and money for movies was hard to come by, so we made our own entertainment. We learned songs at school and later from a battery operated radio, when we could eventually afford one.

The young people of my acquaintance were shy, so romantic gestures took the form of shy glances, and hopeful smiles. Even so you could bet that at these gatherings minds were on the opposite sex. Once in a blue moon there was a party at someone's house where the young people would play games. When the game resulted in a couple being paired they had to go for a walk. Sometimes they would hold hands but that was the only gesture made. They could never be sure another person was not hidden and watching. To be honest the only kiss I had before going away to college was a quick buzz on the cheek from a fellow who walked me home from church.

For the high school prom the committee paired up every one. Sure, the people who had a boy friend were put together. My sister and I were excited over our first evening dress. The boys we were paired with had no car so we spent the night with our uncle who lived near the school and planned to go from there. I don't remember what we did at the prom. It was not a dance because of the strict religious beliefs of the community. The boys who were assigned to be our dates lived in a remote area and did not show up. The prom was a disappointment. We ate our refreshments and went home to our uncle's.

A COUNTRY CHRISTMAS

At Christmas we went serenading. City people call it caroling. We walked from house to house, singing Christmas songs.

We serenaded our neighbors on either side as far as our parents would allow us to go. Neighbors did not live close to each other as today's city or town lots are situated, but a mile or so away. Usually people would give us a piece of candy or fruit.

A few days before Christmas Dad would go into the woods to find a tree. If the weather was good and we were well from colds Mama might let us go with him. Pines were the only suitable trees available so the choice was which pine. It was chosen, cut and brought to the house. The eyes played tricks on us making the trees look much smaller when outside. After some difficulty squeezing it in the door, we invariably found it was too tall for the ceiling and it bent over at the top. Then it had to be squeezed back out the door, cut of at the bottom and squeezed back in again.

When Dad had it set up straight as possible it was time to decorate. We strung popcorn to make garlands. We had saved shiny foil gum wrappers and any other bits of foil we could find all year and made them into icicles. We gathered red holly berries to use for color. We had a homemade cardboard star colored with gold crayon for the top of the tree. We cut out candy canes from the newspaper or from used school paper, colored them with crayons and hung them on the tree. If beauty is in the eye of the beholder our eyes told us the tree was beautiful.

We anticipated the visit of Santa Claus with great excitement. We had looked at the wish book (the Sears catalog) and hoped for wonderful things under the tree on Christmas morning. We hung our stockings, not fancy ones as today but the kind stocking we wore every day. There was no argument about bedtime on Christmas Eve.

Santa never brought all the things we dreamed of. The girls might find a small doll or tea set. The boys would perhaps get a ball, a small truck, or a whistle. The stockings had nuts, candy canes and an orange or apple.

The grown ups in my family did not exchange presents. Only the little ones had a visit from Santa. When children learned of Santa Claus they no longer received gifts under the tree. On looking back, I can scarcely see how our folks treated us as well as they did.

People would often come by to wish us Merry Christmas. It was customary to greet a person by saying, "Christmas gift!" Whoever said it first expected the other to give him a small piece of candy or a nut. If he had none he might find a penny in his pocket to give.

Christmas dinner was no big deal at our house. We were pleased to have dressing with our chicken, baked sweet potato, sweet potato pies or bread pudding. We did not cook for a week as women do today

I have no remembrance of celebrating Thanksgiving at home although we did at school.

Halloween was not a recognized holiday in our section of the country. We didn't celebrate this event. I suppose we heard about it at school but we never knew "trick or treat" during my childhood.

LULLABYS AND CHILDREN'S SONGS

Singing to the babies was another musical outlet, plus it soothed them and lulled them to sleep if it was a lullaby, for example. *Rock-a-bye Baby in the Tree Top* or *Hush Little Baby, Don't Say A Word*. Finger actions usually accompanied limerick songs, such as *Teensy Weensy Spider* and *This Little Piggy Went to Market*. These delighted and stimulated little ones. Older people sang them to us, and we passed them on by singing to younger siblings, nieces, and nephews, or neighbor children.

Older children grew up doing clapping rhymes, yesterday's rap. Two children would rap while clapping hands with each other, "One potato, two potato, three potato, four — five potato six potato seven potato more." There was a set way to clap hands as partners as we played this game. There were also rap-rhythms, which accompanied jumping rope. "Old Mrs. Dingett had big feet. How many biscuits could she eat?" Then count each jump until you missed.

BARNS AND OTHER BUILDINGS

Barns and other out buildings were as important on the farm as the house, maybe more. Our main barn was made with rough planks. On one side were two stalls for the mules, Henry and Kate. The stalls were roofed indoor rooms with a trough for food. They had a dirt floor and the planks used for the walls were spaced far enough apart that we could peek through the cracks. The doors to the stalls were fastened with homemade wooden latches. The stalls opened into a small fenced in area through which a small stream ran; thus water was available. They were fed ears of corn, and fodder each night and closed in their stalls. If it fell our lot to let the mules out to pasture, we made sure to step aside as we opened their door. They were likely to run out rambunctiously.

The middle section of the barn was two stories, the top being the fodder loft. The bottom was the corncrib and storage area for cottonseed meal. This part was more closely built, not having the big cracks between planks as the mule stalls. It had a wooden floor.

On the side opposite the mule stalls was a shed open on both ends under which the wagon and farm tools were kept. On one side of the shed was a row of wooden boxes nailed to the wall about shoulder high and lined with straw. These were hen nests where the hens laid eggs and were "set" on eggs to hatch a brood of chicks. A "setting" hen was not to be disturbed on penalty of being pecked and flogged. She could be very fierce and as children carefully kept our distance, especially after first hand experience.

Behind the corncrib were stalls for the cows. These were similar to the mule stalls. Later Dad built a log cow barn, which had two stalls on each side of an open hall. The pasture was connected to the barn and must have covered several acres. The cows wore bells but they were still hard to find if they chose not to come home at evening milking time.

Sometimes they would get out of the pasture. That made them more difficult to find. They believed the old adage, "The grass is greener on the other side of the fence." Then Dad and my brothers had to walk the fence line to find where it needed repair.

Sometimes when they got out of the pasture, the cows would graze on dog fennel or bitter weed. This made the milk unusable even for cooking. There was no way to remove the bitter taste from the milk. However it was not completely wasted, as the hogs and cats didn't mind the taste.

On one particular occasion that I remember, the milk was bitter and we had used all the canned food. Mama made corn meal mush in the big black pot for supper. It was all we had that night. Water, corn meal, salt, pepper and a little butter made a delicious dish. It was our substitute for grits I suppose, because I never had grits until I went away from home.

The third barn was a storage place for many things. We had a good time playing in this barn. It was closely built with no cracks between the planks. It had a wood floor and partial loft to which we could climb from inside the barn. Cotton was stored here until enough was picked to take to the gin, or perhaps to wait for the price to go up. Extra cotton for quilts and pillows was stored here. It was fun jumping from the loft to the soft cotton, rolling in it and covering each other up. We made sure our feet were clean because Dad did not like dirty cotton.

Other things must have been stored there, which I don't remember. Canned goods were stored with cotton packed around them to keep them from freezing. Buckets of sorghum syrup were kept here.

This barn had a shed at the back, which was used for carpentry and repair work on any thing that needed fixing. Even on rainy days there were chores to be done.

We had a small building we called the smokehouse, though I never knew any meat smoking to be done there. The pork from the hogs was packed in salt to preserve it, in a large box that sat off the dirt floor on two flattened logs. It had a heavy top plus other weights to protect it from any animal thieves. The door to the smokehouse also had a latch that was located up high. The meat kept well until the hot weather of summer came, but by then the best parts had been consumed.

We mustn't forget another small but important building. This one had a seat with two holes and pits dug under the holes. Usually an outdated Sears Roebuck catalog hung on the wall. There was plenty of ventilation, and in the cold of winter the business in this place was conducted as hastily as possible. The outhouse was essential to rural poor people with no indoor pluming, no running water or electricity. Several times a year lime was added to the pits. It kept down any odor and helped to decompose the waste in the pits.

The pigs, or hogs, were housed in something like today's large doghouse, but with no floor. I suppose it could be called a sty. Mostly the pigs lived out side in the pen, but sometimes needed a place to get out of the weather especially when they had piglets. The sty was enclosed by the pigpen. The pigpen had to be built close to the ground because pigs are notorious for rooting under any fenced enclosure.

We were delighted as children when the old sow had a brood of little pink piglets. They were so delightful that we named every one even though they looked so much alike we were never sure we were calling them by the original name.

We never had pet hamsters, rabbits, birds, or any pet of that nature. However we enjoyed the wild birds and tried to identify them. Finding a bird nest was a treasure. We saved the tops of Arm and Hammer baking soda boxes and redeemed them for bird cards. Each card had a picture in color of a certain bird with a description and it's habitat, habits and calls.

TWO ROOM FEDERAL SCHOOL

The second school I attended was upgraded. It had two rooms, which were connected with a removable or sliding wall that could be opened to accommodate a large crowd. Instead of a long bench with desks in front {or you could say on the back) each bench seated two students who shared a double desk. Books, pencils, paper and sometimes lunch was kept in the desk. It was essential that you were compatible with your desk mate or many arguments could arise and often did.

34

The Federal School was so named because it was on Federal Road. Presumably Federal Soldiers had marched this way during the War Between the States. The school was located at least two miles from home. By walking through a path up the hill along beside the pigpen, we were able to cut the distance a little. The old sawmill road, that was now nothing more than a trail, cut off another big curve in the road. It was like going through a forest with huge trees and underbrush all along the path.

This part was scary because of the ghost, which was supposed to walk the trail. The ghost was that of a man, who had been murdered in a fight along the old sawmill road. According to the tale, he was doomed to walk the path until his killer was caught. We sang and made noise that we believed would keep the ghost away.

The walk wasn't too bad most of the time. We walked across our road, which was called Four Mile Road and up the path beside the pigpen to the Federal Road. There some friends usually met us, and we walked the remaining distance together.

When the weather was cold we trampled icicles which were "spewed" up from the ground. Our feet were very cold by the time we reached school. Sometimes long icicles hung from the outcropping of rocks, which were higher than our heads along some sections of the road. We loved to try and climb the slippery rocks to get the longest icicle. This was before pollution and the icicles seemed clean enough for us to enjoy licking them all the way to school.

There was a stream to cross on the way that sometimes became an adventure. There was a foot log across the stream, but most of the time we crossed by stepping on large stones in the creek. Wagons and cars just drove on through the water. It was shallow and they had no shoes to get wet. There were times when we had a "real gully washer" (a great deal of rain). The creek was flooded over its banks and over the foot log out into the road. The older boys would roll up britches legs and carry the little ones through the water.

In contradictory behavior, the older boys would sometimes go earlier, climb up trees along the haunted path or otherwise hide. When we came along they would make animal noises or eerie ghost noises to scare us. We would run the rest of the way to school, scared "spitless."

With all this fun on the way to school it is surprising that we were not late quite often. However, the school bell rang at a "quarter 'til," and again at "books," which was the time to be seated at our desks and be quiet. The bell was a large farm bell on a post by the schoolhouse door and could be heard for miles. If we were not near school when we heard the first bell we had to run as fast as we could to avoid being late.

Mrs. Beulah Fann's room held the first four grades, (which included primer) and Mrs. Davis taught fourth, fifth, sixth and seventh. When I had reached fifth grade Mr. Christian came to teach those grades. The first names of both teachers elude me.

Students held the teachers in great respect and some fear. The teachers were free to use a paddle or a hickory switch. Only the boldest students misbehaved or disobeyed. As punishment for talking or giggling, considered minor infractions, we were made to stand in the corner. Chewing gum was not allowed. It was not uncommon to find a wad stuck inside the desk, hidden there when a student was near to being caught with it.

We had conservative, responsible parents who always thought the teacher was right. We knew that if we were paddled or switched at school we could expect likewise when we got home. Some other child or sibling was bound to tell. Parents always knew what went on at school, especially our parents.

When it was time for a class to recite, we brought the appropriate book and sat on the front row. This was true for any subject. Reading, English, spelling, arithmetic, Georgia history, and geography were the third grade subjects. It was always fun when we were allowed to do arithmetic problems on the blackboard. We did a lot of board work and oral questions and answers because of the need to conserve paper. There was probably no shortage of paper but shortage of money to buy paper.

Schoolbooks were furnished by this time. They belonged to the school and students were required to turn them in at the end of the year. It was necessary to take good care of them so other students who were advancing to that grade the next year could use them.

Geography must have been my most difficult subject in the third grade. I had many years of teasing about my answer to the question "What is the most prolific product in Georgia?" My answer was, "Rocks." It was surmised that because of the difficulty of hoeing cotton and corn with so many rocks in the field and the unfortunate incidents of 'stumping' bare toes on rocks, I, nearing the age of nine, reached my conclusion that rocks were the most numerous product of Georgia.

We had quite a lot of homework. We helped each other by calling the spelling words out and checking them, listening to each other recite the multiplication tables and listening to a reading lesson. We tried to study before dark. This was possible if we didn't have to work in the fields or do other chores after school. Daylight was better to study by than the light of a kerosene lamp.

When another class was reciting we were expected to study at our seats. However any excuse to get out of our seats was welcome. Sometimes two people were chosen, usually because they were well behaved, to go outside and dust blackboard erasers, or wash the blackboards. We had no janitor therefore we had the privilege of sweeping the wooden floors, which had been treated with some kind of oil, to keep down the dust, I suppose. We also emptied trashcans and in winter we brought in wood for the pot bellied stove. In winter we wore coats all day because of the inefficient heat of the stove.

Friday afternoons were always exciting and fun. We took a break from regular classes. We had spelling bees, and number drills, which we didn't think of as studying. Sometimes our teacher would read us stories such as *Huckleberry Finn* and *Tom Sawyer* or *Treasure Island*. We had no library at the school. Our teacher checked out the books from the county library and brought them to read to us.

There was a stage on one end of the room. The blackboard was at the back of it, so we had to go on the stage to write on the blackboard. Sometimes we did skits on the stage. At Christmas each child learned a poem or reading for a program to which parents were invited. Here is one that I remember.

"Mama won't you darn my stocking,
Foot is peeping through the toe.
Santa Claus would find it shocking,
If he should find it so."

Great fun was always in store at recess. Recess was a favorite time at school, especially when the weather was warm. Lunch was fun too, because we had time for games. We hurried through eating lunch in order to have time to play games.

Lunch was usually a sibling affair, as one lunch pail, a recycled lard bucket, was packed for all the children in the family. We had ham or jelly biscuits, with occasionally a cookie or fried apple tart, and sometimes a baked sweet potato. For some reason we never made yeast breads nor bought them. Therefore we had no sandwiches.

The only drink we had was water, which some of the older children drew from the well at the Bozeman house across the road. We had no spring or well at the school. We did have outhouses, one for the girls and one for the boys.

Some of the games we played were Kick the Can, Stealing Sticks, Red Rover, Antney Over, Bum-Bum-Bum, and of course baseball, when someone would bring a home made ball and bat. The ball was made of rubber from an old inner tube, sewn together to make the inside. The outside was then wrapped with yarn from old stockings that had been unraveled. It had to be sewn to keep it from coming off. Even so the ball often had a streamer of yarn hanging from it. After Christmas someone might have a rubber ball that Santa had brought. Those wore out rapidly with much use. The bat was a piece of three or four-inch wide plank that had been chiseled or carved narrow at one end to form a handle. It left splinters in our hands if not smooth..

Antny Over was played with children choosing up sides. One side stationed themselves on each side of the schoolhouse. The side with the ball would call out Antny Over and throw the ball over the schoolhouse. Someone caught the ball, then the team ran around the side of the school and tagged as many people as he could by touching them with the ball. All those who were tagged had to remain on the side of the person who tagged them. Nobody knew who had the ball or which side of the building they would be coming around. They tried to run around to the other side without being tagged. Then it was the other side's turn to throw the ball. The object was to end up with all players on your side, hence winning the game.

The object of Red Rover was the same, but the game was different. The two sides lined up facing each other, about twenty-five feet apart. The first side held hands to make a solid line and called all together, "Red Rover, Red Rover, send Tom (or whomever they chose) over." He ran as fast as he could into the arms between two people trying to break through. If he was successful he could choose someone to carry back to his side. If not, then he had to stay on this side. It is amazing that someone didn't get a broken arm, because large and small children played together. This game could be painful and left most with red, sore arms. Crack the Whip was another rough game.

Bum-Bum-Bum was also played with each side facing at about twenty-five or thirty feet. Each side drew a line three feet in front of their line with a stick in the dirt and they were ready to play. This was a game of pantomime. The team, whose turn it was, decided on some action such as churning, or climbing a tree. They would march to the first line and chant; "Bum-Bum-Bum here we come." The second side; "What's your trade?" First side; "sweet lemonade." Second side; "Get to work and get it made." The first side would then pantomime the action they had planned while the opposition guessed what it was. When someone guessed correctly the first team was chased back to its baseline and any one caught had to remain on the catcher's team. Nobody was ever out of the game. They just had to change sides, so everyone got to keep playing.

Stealing Sticks was similar. Each side had a circle with a certain number of sticks in it. Both sides tried to steal the other teams sticks and if they were caught they had to change sides. The game was over when one side was out of sticks.

I don't know where these games originated. I suppose they were handed down from one generation to another. They were very popular with all the children.

One event held at the school is very dim in my memory, perhaps because it was held before I was old enough to participate and was discontinued later. The event was Box Suppers. I remember my older sisters getting ready for it. It was both a social and a fund raising project. Young ladies eagerly decorated a box with colorful bits of ribbon, cloth, lace, and rickrack. They worked many days to make it attractive. On the day of the supper the most delicious food the young lady could cook was packed in the box. It was carried to the supper under cover, so no one knew who packed any box. The young men did their best to find out, because they had favorites. You see, they were to bid on the box, and the highest bidder also won the right to share supper with the young lady. In those days, if someone bid over a dollar it was considered a high priced supper and the young lady was very flattered. The money was used for some school need.

When I was in the sixth or seventh grade we took a trip to Atlanta on the school bus. I suppose it was my first bus ride. Parents and siblings not in school were invited as chaperons and caretakers. Each person paid admission fee to the Cyclorama, and zoo. The Cyclorama is a realistic circular panorama of the battle of Atlanta. Figures of soldiers and horses appeared in all sorts of battle poses. The display of artillery, cannons and rifles with bayonets was very realistic. You felt you could almost reach out and touch the dead, wounded and weary soldiers. It was not discernible where the display of figures ended and the scenes continued in a panoramic painting. The show was done with lights, sound and music. It was the only one of its kind at that time. It was an amazing marvelous experience to all of us country kids who had never even seen a movie. This trip was considered part of our history lesson.

Seeing the animals in the zoo was just as thrilling. The pictures we had seen only in books become real live creatures, with sounds and scents. It was an exciting day.

We attended Federal School through the seventh grade. When we were promoted to eighth grade we were considered in high school and rode the bus to school.

FARM ANIMALS - PETS?

Farm animals to a farmer were like sunshine is to plants, a necessity. As children we considered all the farm animals pets. We named the cows and new calves, the pigs too, even though we knew the pigs would eventually be pork chops and the calves sold. The cows and calves were very "petable" with their big brown eyes and loved to have their nose and neck rubbed. We could hold out feed in our hand and they would lick it up. We also liked to hold out a long stalk of corn for the mules, being careful to take our hand away before they nibbled to the end.

Once a year the county vet came around inspecting our cows and giving them necessary shots or medication to prevent disease. This prevented them transmitting any disease to us. To continue producing milk the cows had to be bred and birth a calf. Most people had no bull, so when the time was right the cow had to be driven to a neighbor who had one. This chore belonged to the men of the family.

Sometimes the calf was sold and sometimes kept to replace the old cow and she was sold.

I hardly think it would have been possible to survive on the farm without chickens. They served as the meat and eggs for our table as well as barter at the store. Chickens and hens had full freedom to roam the yard and needless to say we had to be careful where we stepped.

We didn't name all the chickens. There were too many I suppose, and they were not very "petable." Still it was pleasant to hold a soft fluffy yellow chick in our hands. Mostly they were aloof except at feeding time, when we scattered corn on the ground. They would fight over it. Sometimes we mixed cornmeal and water to make a crumbly batter to feed the biddies and young chicks. We did call the hens by their breed name, "old Dominecker hen has stolen her nest," we might say. We had White Leghorns, Rhode Island Reds, and the Dominicks, which were black and white striped, much like a zebra. Occasionally we would have a hen that would never lay eggs in the nest boxes, but would "steal her nest" and we always had to hunt for it. Needless to say she usually ended up in the stew pot.

In the spring when a hen "took a notion to set," we would mark about a dozen eggs and put in her nest. She would incubate them constantly except for eating and water breaks. When the eggs hatched in about three weeks she had a good brood. We were always excited about the little chicks hatching and kept a close watch on the nest. After they hatched they followed the mother hen around the yard until they learned to eat and take care of themselves. If anything frightened her or seemed dangerous to her chicks she gathered them under her wings hiding them and protecting them. When you saw her sitting there you could not believe ten chicks were underneath her.

We never knew how many chicks would be roosters and how many hens. We couldn't tell until they were older and their feathers grew. We kept only one rooster or maybe two. All the others ended up in the frying pan, or traded at the store.

THE PERSONALITY OF MULES

The mules were named Henry and Kate. They enjoyed having their face stroked and neck scratched. We were very careful to stay away from their backsides, however, as we never knew when they would decide to kick. Mules' back feet could pack quite a wallop, and serious injury could occur. Henry and Kate were pretty even tempered and never gave us any trouble in that respect. They were seen kicking at dogs when the dogs followed too close barking or nipping at their heels. The dogs hightailed it out of the way. The mules regularly switched their tails at flies that bothered them in summer. If a person chanced to be in the way the tail could deliver a swat that could hurt.

Henry and Kate had different personalities or temperaments. Henry was docile and calm, not easily excited. Kate was skittery, easily startled and sometimes unpredictable. One day when I had fed the mules and let them out in the pasture I failed to fasten the pasture gate securely. Henry got out of the pasture and I started after him to try to get him back inside. While I was chasing him Kate got out too. I was scolded thoroughly for chasing him instead of fastening the gate so Kate couldn't get out. The idea was that Henry was easier to catch than Kate and much easier than both together.

I waited fearfully for Dad to get the mules up thinking I was due a heavy punishment. To my great surprise I had only a scolding and admonishment never to allow it to happen again.

The mules were needed to pull the wagon and plows, harrows and other farm machinery. None of our neighbors had a farm tractor. If there were farm tractors at that time we had no means of buying one. Mules were vital to farming in those days.

It was a special treat when Dad would let us ride a mule home from a hard day's work in the field. There was no saddle, and we had to hold on to the collar, and rope that was part of the gear used to hitch the mule to the plow. The sweaty odor of the mule didn't bother us. To be honest there were many odors we encountered on the farm that would not be acceptable today.

IT'S A DOG'S LIFE

We always had dogs and cats. Although we enjoyed petting them neither were primarily pets. The dogs were expected to chase rabbits, squirrels and other animals from the garden and yard, and out of the barn where the corn and feed were stored. They were to keep foxes away from hens and chickens. They were also used to hunt. My folks never hunted deer or quail that I remember. Neither did they fish. They hunted rabbit, squirrel and possum. We often had rabbit or squirrel stew or dumplings.

Dad was always after Mama to cook possum. Only once do I remember Mama doing so. Once was enough. She said they were nothing but grease and greased up the whole kitchen. This was one thing Dad could not change her mind about.

After much begging my brothers finally agreed to let me go possum hunting with them. Possum season was in the fall when the weather was crisp and cool and the leaves crunched under foot. Wild persimmons were ripe on the trees. A lantern was carried deep into the woods. The glow was pleasant but eerie and only lit a short area around it. A fire was built to keep warm and scare off bears, or so they told me. (I now know there were no bears in that part of the country.) Everyone sat around the fire, listening to the dogs barking as they chased, and waiting for them to tree a possum. This was a good time to tell ghost stories and get little sister very, very scared. Certainly children and young people delight in being scared. Look at all the horror movies out today.

If the dogs treed a possum it was usually up a small persimmon tree. Then my brothers shook the tree vigorously until the possum fell out onto the ground, curled up and played dead causing the dogs to lose interest. Since Mama refused to cook it I suppose they let it go. Sometimes they would bring it home holding it by the tale to show it off.

Any time we misbehaved we were told that a "Booger" would get us. Often I would neglect my chores, such as bringing in wood or bringing up water for the night until it was dark. Then I would call the dog, named Bowzer, to go with me so that I wouldn't be scared. I'm told that I was heard chanting "Booger bite Bowzer, Bowzer bite him" over and over. I didn't know what a Booger was, but knew that it was something terrible and frightening.

All the dogs we had from time to time were mixed breeds, hounds, beagles, and various unknowns. Bowzer was probably the nearest dog to being just a pet that we had. His color was sort of reddish gold and white and from his looks he must have been part Collie. None of the dogs were allowed in the house, but Bowzer was desperately afraid of thunder and lightening. From the first clap of thunder he would somehow get into the house and

44

under the bed he would go. There was no getting him out until the storm was over.

We bought no dog food, probably had never heard of it. Dogs were expected to catch some of their own food, but were fed some left over bread and meat scraps They could always enjoy gnawing the soup bones when they were ready to be discarded,

THE SKUNK IN THE RABBIT TRAP

Dad often made and set rabbit boxes (traps). I suppose the dogs we had at the time were not good rabbit dogs or perhaps the rabbits were getting into the garden to which the dogs hadn't access. The traps were wooden with a door that closed when a trigger inside was tripped. I don't remember what he baited them with. Sometimes other animals were caught in the traps. On one occasion when Dad checked the trap he found he had caught a skunk.

He brought the box into the yard and all the children and adults peeped into the hole in the top to see the skunk. It really was beautiful, all shiny black fur with the white stripe down his back. We didn't understand then why he didn't spray his scent, but after studying, we knew that he had to be able to raise his tail, and the box was too small to allow him to do this. There was the problem of getting him out of the box. If it was opened and he was shooed out, he would certainly let loose his spray. We had known times when the dogs got into it with a skunk and we couldn't stand to have them around for weeks. Finally someone came up with the idea of taking box and skunk to the creek and holding it under water until the skunk drowned. I remember regretting that such a pretty animal should end in that manner, but he probably had plenty of brothers and sisters in the woods nearby to replace him. Anyhow the strategy worked.

THE CAT AND THE MICE

The duty of the farm cat was to catch mice. They were barn cats and their primary source of food was rats and mice.

45

Cute little kittens were sometimes given milk. Grown cats were rarely given milk. They were expected to catch their dinner. They lived mostly outside or in the barn, especially in the corncrib and where corn and the cottonseed meal was kept. Sometimes a cat would develop an affinity for catching the little chicks. Needless to say he had to be disposed of. Cats were seldom allowed in the house. They sometimes curled up to sun on the porch, and some were tame enough to hold and pet. Later, after I had moved away, Mama had a black cat of which she was very fond. This cat was allowed in the house and given generous portions of milk.

CHORES

One of the primary daily chores to be done year-round was feeding the animals and milking the cows. Dad or the boys usually fed the mules and hogs. My oldest sister Lenora usually did the milking, This chore was done morning and night. I learned to milk and helped her often, and sometimes substituted for her if she was not feeling well. I liked the cows and was never afraid of them. Some of my sisters were scared of them, which we told them was just an excuse to get out of a chore they didn't like. As sisters do, we had our quarrels.

The milk was brought to the house and strained. The strainer and milk buckets had to be scalded with boiling water to sterilize them each time they were used. When the weather was very cold the milk sometimes formed ice crystals in it when left in the kitchen over night. If the weather was warm the milk was taken to the spring box. This was the refrigerator of the era.

The milk we did not drink went into the churn to clabber. Churning was one job I did not like. My nature was averse to sitting in one place very long, and it seemed forever before the butter came. There was a rhyme we used to chant while churning. "Come butter, come. Mama's waiting at the gate, to make a sweet butter cake. Come butter, come. Come butter come."

The butter was lifted from the milk carefully with the dasher. Then water was worked through it two or three times to get all the buttermilk out. Salt was worked into the butter. Sometimes it was molded in a pretty mold especially if we expected company, but other times it was just mounded in a plate.

The buttermilk was cooled in the springbox. Country people loved to drink buttermilk with their vegetables and corn bread. Some of my family liked crumbling corn bread into their buttermilk and eating it with a spoon. Buttermilk was used in cooking all breads and cakes. The butter was used to make cakes but lard was used for breads.

Margarine and vegetable cooking oil were not produced at that time. The first margarine was produced during WWII. It was white and came with an envelope of color that had to be mixed to make it resemble butter. The taste was very flat and no one who had the real thing would think of using it as a substitute.

THE SPRING BOX

To keep milk and butter from spoiling in the summer we kept it in the spring box. Our water all came from a clear spring that bubbled from the ground. It was quite cool. The spring box sat in the water just below the spring. It had holes in each end so the water could flow continuously through it and around the milk. It had a leather fastener that fitted around a wooden button securely to keep animals out. Butter and buttermilk was also kept in the spring box.

In summer the spring box also held watermelons. I haven't had melon since those days that was as good as spring-cooled melon. Many times we had neighbors over for a watermelon cutting. Dad made a big production of this. He set the melon on a shelf on the back porch or on a makeshift table in the yard. Wielding the butcher knife he sliced it into individual slices. We ate these by holding them in our hands and biting into them. It was quite messy with juice running down our chin we needed to lean forward to keep from dripping it on our clothes. The seeds were spit upon the ground where sooner or later the chickens or birds found a treat. Sometimes we had a contest to see who could spit the seeds farther.

The melons we "busted" and ate when we worked in the fields were even more delicious. I suppose the fact we were hot and thirsty helped the taste. At mid-afternoon rest time when we were hot and tired from picking cotton, Dad or our older sister would give us permission to bust a melon. We bumped it on a rock, pulled it apart where it cracked and broke pieces off by bumping the halves on the rock. Needless to say we had a lot of juice running down our chins as we ate by holding it to our mouth and eating it from the uneven rind. We always had a bucket of drinking water with us in the fields and could wash our hands. Some fields were near a stream, which was available for washing up.

If Dad or the older boys were with us their pocketknife came in handy for cutting the melon and made eating less messy. We had red and yellow meat watermelons. I always thought the yellow were sweeter. These days when we get everything from the supermarket I never see a yellow meat watermelon.

CHOPPING WOOD

Other daily chores were chopping wood, which Dad and my brothers usually did. Trees were cut and the logs trimmed and dragged from the woods. Cutting trees served two purposes. They provided "new ground" for a cotton or corn patch and wood for heating and cooking. The trees were cut into fireplace or stove wood lengths with the crosscut saw. Some times the men were off and busy when wood was needed. Then we pitched in and manned the saw or split the wood for the stove. Bringing it into the house was always a chore that belonged to us children. A box near the stove was filled with wood for cooking. Each day the ashes were cleaned out of the stove. The ashes were put on the garden to help the soil. There were logs for the fireplace in winter and kindling to be brought in. A lot of splinters were gathered in tender fingers from the wood. We learned to watch out for them.

COOL CLEAR WATER

If people did not have a cool bubbling spring of water they had a well from which to draw water. We were fortunate to have a clear cool natural spring as our source of water. Another chore assigned to us kids was bringing up the water from the spring. Usually two large buckets of water were brought to the house each evening. This water was for cooking, drinking, washing dishes, and hands. Sponge baths were the usual way of bathing, especially in the winter. People didn't think they had to have a bath every day. Soap and water were used sparingly, as people do today when camping. Octagon brand soap was what we used for washing just about everything, sometimes even ourselves.

Our hand and bath soap of record was the old red bar of Lifebuoy soap, which had a slight Lysol scent. If my older sisters had some money to spend they would sometimes indulge in a pure white bar of Ivory. They were very stingy with it and sometimes hid it from the younger children.

I have one faint remembrance of making lye soap, but we didn't use homemade soap as a rule. It was a complicated production. You needed lye, a very caustic substance, and a lot of fat or lard. It was heated carefully in the wash pots, put out to cool and cut into bars. Cleaning up must have been difficult. The family thought it was not worth the trouble.

SATURDAY SPECIALS

On Saturday afternoon in warm weather water was heated in the big black iron wash pots and we took turns bathing in the washtubs outside. We could fill the washtub with water, set it in the sun and the water would be warm enough to bathe in. We made a bath tent by draping a dark cloth over a corner of the clothesline. Mama or our older sister would make sure we scrubbed good and didn't miss any spots, behind our ears for example.

Sometimes we went to the creek to bathe. The water was quite chilly at first, so we sat down slowly to ease into it. This was a wonderfully pleasant venture on a hot summer day. The creek was not deep enough to swim but it was fun to splash in the cool water. Quite a distance down stream my brothers found a place deep enough to swim. It remains a mystery why the girls didn't go there.

Saturday was barbershop day. Dad had a pair of hand clippers and lined the boys up for a haircut when they began to look shaggy The clippers could pinch and the hair fell down their neck into their shirt making them itch in spite of the cloth Dad had hung around their neck. Cutting five heads of hair took most of the afternoon.

Scissors were used to cut the girls' hair. Mama or an older sister did the honors. The style was a straight cut around the back and straight bangs across the forehead. Later I learned it is called a pageboy cut. If our bangs were down in our eyes it was time for a trim. An old wive's tale said that hair in your eyes made you cross-eyed. We took no chances!

We had curling irons that were heated on the stove or fire. If too hot it could scorch the hair and oh the smell! Shirley Temple curls were the result of curling irons. This curled the hair for one day if the weather was not damp. If the day was rainy the curl was usually gone by the time we arrived at school. During my high school days women began to get permanent waves. They were called "permanent" even though the wave lasted about three months.

Permanent wave machines looked like a torture device. The tress of hair was covered with a piece of tissue paper and rolled on a metal roller. Next it was heavily padded between the curler and the head. A protective pad was placed on the metal curler. A heavy electric attachment was clamped on each curl. By this time the head was so heavy one could hardly hold it up. The electric heat was turned on. The timing was critical. If left too long it would burn the hair, if too little time no curl would be the result. I had one permanent wave with this machine after which I said "never again." I preferred straight hair to this procedure.

WASHDAY - BLUE MONDAY

Monday was washday. With such a large family, it was an all day job. One of my older sisters was in charge, either Lenora or Thenia. I loved to help in the summer because it meant I was excused from working in the field. In the winter our hands felt like they were turning blue with cold when we did the wash. There were times when the wet wash froze on the line before the day was warm enough to dry it.

The wash place was purposely located just below the spring. The first job was to fill the two large iron wash pots with water and build a fire under them. While the water heated we went back to the house and gathered and sorted the clothes. We put whites in the tub and combined the hot water with cold, scrubbing the clothes by hand. We rubbed Octagon soap on any spots and then scrubbed them on the tin washboard. Later we progressed to Lux Soap Flakes and felt we were moving on up the ladder.

After washing we wrung the water out with wrist action and put them in one of the wash pots to boil. We punched them up occasionally with the "battling" stick. This was a wooden paddle, homemade and smoothed, with which we "battled" or beat very soiled or greasy overalls or other garments. These particular garments were too heavy to effectively scrub by hand or wash board. We had what we called a "battling" stump, actually a piece of log turned on end. After we wet and soaped the clothes we put them on the stump and beat them with the paddle, turning them so that every part was treated. One person did this while the other washed the less dirty colored clothes.

By this time the whites were ready to take out of the pot to rinse in fresh, clean cold water. They were removed from the boiling water with the battling stick one at a time and carried to the tub on the wash bench. Care had to be taken in summer not to drip boiling water on bare feet or legs.

Next the colored clothes went into the pot to boil. Many times there was a light color and a dark color wash that made three loads. While the colored boiled, the whites were rinsed through two tubs of clean water, and wrung out to be hung on the clothesline.

The clothesline had to be wiped clean. It was usually part in sun and part in shade and was attached to two trees. The white clothes were hung in the sun, colors in the shade.

Starch was made up for dress shirts and dresses. This was done by boiling flour and water together. It was very thick and had to be thinned with cold water. Sunday shirts, Sunday dresses and school dresses were starched before hanging on the line.

There were a few delicate Sunday dresses of voile or pique, and sweaters that received more tender treatment. But for the most part clothes were made of durable cotton fabric.

When all the clothes were finished and hung, the pots and tubs had to be emptied and rinsed. The tubs were turned upside down on the wash bench and the fire doused.

When dry, the clothes were folded directly from the line. Sheets and pillowcases were returned to the beds as we had only one set per bed, except for the good "company" sheets. Sun dried sheets had a wonderfully fresh smell.

Starched clothes were sprinkled with water and then rolled up so they would become evenly damp. Ironing was a hot job in summer. We used the old black flat irons heated on the kitchen stove. While one was used the other was on the stove to heat. Later, we had an iron that was filled with charcoal and lighted to heat. This was much more comfortable in the summer than firing up the stove to heat the irons. Advantage too, the iron did not need reheating.

We ironed on the table padded with an old quilt and covered with a sheet. My sisters argued about which side of the garment should be ironed first, because the first side became wrinkled again, sometimes, when it was turned over to iron the second side. Ironing boards eliminated this problem.

CANE BOTTOM CHAIRS

In early spring when the oak tree saplings were tender and pliable, Dad would cut them and strip the inner part splitting it very thin for use in weaving new bottoms for the cane-bottomed ladder-backed chairs. The strips were moist and supple but would become tight when they dried. There was an art to weaving the bottoms into the chairs. My sister learned to do this but I never did. It was fascinating to watch.

MAKING SEDGE BROOMS

A seasonal chore was making brooms from tall sedge grass. When it dried in the fall, handfuls were twisted off close to the ground. When enough was gathered the sedge was wound and tied together with a string. The broom was much shorter than the wooden handled brooms of today. When it was new, the sweeping end was soft and pliable, and was perfect for sweeping the wood floors of the house. When worn it became short and stubby, which made it perfect for sweeping the yard. We had no grass, just dirt and sand. I don't know why weeds and some kind of grass did not grow. Today it seems that nature abhors a bare space Weeds and grass grow every where you don't want them. Our bare yard needed sweeping of any sticks, chicken droppings or other debris. We usually did this on Saturday so it would be clean for any Sunday company.

SCRUBBING AND SCOURING

Scrubbing and scouring was a once a year chore, done usually in the spring, or perhaps when the crops were laid by. It was an all day chore from early morning until late afternoon. Every thing in the house was moved outside, except the kitchen stove. The iron beds and springs were taken apart and placed outside to be scalded. All things made of cloth, pillows, quilts and feather beds were put on the line or in the sun to air. Water was heated in the wash pots, and buckets of scalding soapy water were splashed on the walls, and floors of the house. The floors were scrubbed with a broom made of broomsedge. After the soap scrubbing, everything was rinsed with cold water.

The fireplace was cleaned of ashes and scrubbed, and later whitewashed. I don't know what mineral the whitewash was made of. We gathered it from a bank in the road near the creek and mixed it with water to make a paste. We painted it on the large rough rocks of which the fireplace was made. It covered all the smoke-darkened places and looked very fresh and clean.

All our beds were made of iron. The beds and bedsprings were scalded outside. The "bed tics" (or mattress covers) were washed and filled with fresh straw before returning them to the beds. They were fun to sleep on when they were freshly filled because the straw was soft and fluffy and very high. After a while it would compact and not be as comfortable. The pillows were filled with cotton. Mama was the only one who had a feather bed. Later my older sister inherited grandma's featherbed. There were funny stories told about grandma picking feathers from her pet geese to stuff the bed.

By the time we got everything back in, and the beds back together, the house smelled all fresh and nice. I suspect this practice of "scrub and scouring" was partly to prevent bedbugs or to get rid of them. As more upholstered furniture was acquired, this practice was discontinued. Some other way, such as spraying had to be found to combat bugs. The old fashioned way was probably healthier and smelled a heap better.

PLANTING - SPRING AND SUMMER CHORES

Spring planting was more work for the men of the family than the women. I don't remember helping with the planting of the vegetable garden, but remember vividly "toting" guano, cottonseed and corn seed.

Preparing the field for planting was hard work. Dad and my brothers worked behind the mules and plow, turning the ground, harrowing it smooth, and then laying off the rows. Mid morning and mid afternoon found us kids carrying a bucket of water to the field so they could have a refreshing drink.

When the ground was ready one mule was hitched to the guano spreader and the other to the planter. As Dad and one of my brothers walked behind and guided the mules, it was our job to keep the hopper filled. We stood at the end of the row at the edge of the field beside the sacks of seed and fertilizer. We had to be alert and have a bucket of seeds or guano ready when they came to the end of the row, or depending on the length of the field, more or less often. Later we acquired a planter that had a double hopper and could put down fertilizer and seed in one operation. The hoppers could be adjusted to put the right amount as needed into a previously laid furrow, and a single wing plow situated somewhat to the rear of the hoppers covered the seed. The single hopper was adjustable also, but could put down only one thing at a time. This long ago farm equipment is now in museums.

We could catch "what for" if we were not ready to fill the hopper when needed. Neither Dad, nor any of my brothers ever cursed or very, very rarely used any dirty words. Still they could give us a wordy, angry lecture, a "tongue-lashing," which made us very unhappy. We tried as hard as possible to avoid this.

The strongest language I ever heard my dad use was expressions such as: Dad burn it, dad gum it, dog gone it, dern it, the dang thing, and drat! This was mostly when he was plowing a new ground where the plow was running into roots, stumps, and becoming tangled with vines. He also let out one of these expressions when he happened to hit his finger with the hammer. We never used the dirty four-letter word unless it was necessary, for example if we had stepped in it, or were warning someone else to "look out and don't step in it!" Language can be very interesting and expressive without the use of offensive words.

Corn and cotton were the main crops planted. Cotton was the cash crop and corn was the survival crop. I don't remember our family ever planting wheat, but my sisters say they do. Guess that was before I came along.

Other crops were small fields of sorghum, Irish and sweet potatoes, melons, and the garden vegetables that were planted in a fenced area.

Seed Irish potatoes were bought and readied for planting by cutting them into pieces so that each piece had an eye. We carefully placed the piece into the furrow so the eye was up. (Or was it down?) Then they were covered with the plow, or the hoe, if the plow was being used elsewhere.

Sweet potatoe "slips" had to be set out by hand on a mounded bed. The ground was prepared with the plows. Then we had an assembly line operation for planting. One person went down the row making holes with a hoe. The second person put a slip in each hole. A third person carried a bucket of water and gourd and poured water in the hole. The next person pulled the dirt up around the slip, sometimes by hand, sometimes with a hoe. I always thought the watering was the hardest part, because water had to be brought from the spring or branch, quite a distance, depending on where Dad decided the potato patch should be that year.

By the time we got all the crops in the ground, the first crop had "come up," (germinated into seedlings), along with many weeds and grass. Farm chores were never ending. There was more work to be done weeding and thinning the plants.

Pulling up the extra stalks thinned the corn. It could not be chopped off or it would continue to grow, and be too crowded to produce. If there were skips in the row where the seed had not come up, replanting was done at this time.

Most of the corn was planted in the bottomland near the creek where the soil was more fertile. Weeding between plants in the row was done with a hoe. The weeds and grass between rows, in the middles, was plowed up. A plow attachment that Dad called a middle buster was used for this job. When laying by time was approaching, the soil was plowed so that it was piled fairly high around the corn. Even so, when spring rains came in abundance the creek would overflow it's banks into the cornfield washing the corn to the ground. We spent many hours after a rain, bare foot in the mud straightening up the corn with a hoe and hands.

I remember one rainy spring when Dad complained that we hoed the weeds and grass into the middles, the rain set it out to continue growing; but when they plowed the middles, the grass was turned back into the rows and continued to grow there. It was a no win situation.

Cotton was chopped with a hoe to thin. A hoe's width was left between each plant. The same procedure for weeding was done as for corn. However the cotton plants were very delicate and we had to be very careful not to cut them down when weeding. We wore no gloves and wielding the hoe often left us with blistered hands early in spring before our hands toughened.

The clothing we wore for work in the fields was protective from the sun as well as briars. The men wore overalls, long sleeved shirts and straw hats. Dad had an old suede hat that he wore. My older sisters wore fairly long dresses and sunbonnets. Later we younger girls were allowed to wear old overalls, but only in the fields. Ladies never wore pants in public back then. Women, until World War II, did not wear pants in public. When they worked in the bomber plants and had to climb into precarious positions, pants were necessary. Loose dresses were a hazard in the work place, as they could become caught in the machinery. This started a whole new trend in women's wear!

I didn't like the sunbonnets and Mama would often find me without mine. She would say, "Put on that bonnet. You'll be as brown as an Indian!" Suntans were undesirable. A lady was expected to have a white complexion. We had no black people living anywhere near us and seldom saw one in town either. Apparently Mama was more familiar with Indians who must have lived in the area when she was growing up.

When the crops grew too big for working in them, it was "laying by" time. Continued plowing and hoeing would injure the roots. This was a slack time on the farm, and was usually about the first of July. This slack time during our grammar school years was occupied by six weeks of school, which was needed to make a complete year. Children were needed to help with the harvest in the fall so school was not in session. For six weeks during September and/or October we were busy picking cotton, and gathering corn and fodder.

SNOW WHITE COTTON FIELDS

Around late September or early October the cotton bolls opened and the fields became white. Time to hit the road with the pick sack. Dad always said the cool nights and warm days caused the cotton to open. It certainly seemed that the weather was a factor.

My oldest sister, Lenora, was the "field general." When we worked in the fields, she said when and how long we could rest at break time and when it was quitting time. Both were judged by where the sun was in the sky. Incredibly she could tell within fifteen minutes the time of day by the sun. We had no watch to look at. Dad had a pocket watch but he was not always in the same field as we were.

We had one field that was far enough away from the house that we took our lunch, in addition to the bucket of water we usually carried. Too much time was wasted if we walked all the way home and back for lunch. Even though we put the lunch and water in the shade, the water was quite warm to drink. However anything wet was refreshing during a hot day's work in the cotton or corn patch. It was restful to eat a buttered jelly biscuit and potato in the shade. Then we could lie down on our back to rest a while, watching the white fleecy clouds move across the blue sky and trying to spot shapes of animals, ships or other objects in them.

Each of us had our own pick sack for picking cotton. This was made of a tow sack. It was a burlap bag that once held cottonseed or some other product. We added a strap, (usually made from "galluses" which were the shoulder straps of worn out overalls), to go over our head and shoulder. It was adjusted according to the height of the person to whom it belonged. The strap was closer together on one side to allow the sack to sag a bit in the front. This allowed a handful of cotton to be more easily stuffed into the opening. It was worn to one side of the back.

Picking cotton was back breaking work. Stooping for hours would sometimes put a crick in our back. As young people we recovered very quickly and forgot it as soon as we were free to play. Older people were not so fortunate. It bothered them longer.

The cotton bolls had sharp points on them, and many times we pricked our fingers. There was another annoyance that I dreaded more and tried to watch out for and avoid. This was a big, fat, green worm covered with prickly looking spines and having horns on its head. When touched, they stung leaving a red mottled burning spot on the hand or finger. It seemed forever before this ceased to hurt.

Occasionally we would encounter a snake under the cotton stalks. No one was ever bitten that I remember which is incredible seeing as how we were outdoor people and ran barefoot through the yard at night to catch lightning bugs. When we encountered a snake in the field we called the dog to "sic 'em" on the snake. At least one dog was always with us in the field. If he hadn't gone off chasing a rabbit, he was usually in the shade asleep, in a place where he had dug the ground to a cool level. He would bark furiously and grab the snake by the neck just behind the head, then shake it very hard, turning it loose at just the right time so that it landed three or four feet away. Then go grab it again unless it was fast enough to race away. The battle sometimes ended with a dead snake.

We tried to turn work into fun. We sang and harmonized while we worked. We also raced each other to see who could finish picking his or her row first. When our pick sacks were full we emptied them into a larger sack at the end of the row. Sometimes we had a contest to see who could pick the most cotton in a day. Then each one emptied his pick sack into his own sack at the end of the row. I was never able to pick quite a hundred pounds in a day. At the end of the day the sacks were weighed and emptied into the wagon to which the side panels had been added. Riding home lying on top of the soft cotton after a long day's work was heavenly.

If we were caught up with our own cotton harvest, a neighbor, who perhaps had no children, might hire us to pick for him at 10 cents a pound. We could usually earn about 90 cents in a day, and we were very pleased with this. It would be enough to order material from Sears Roebuck for a new dress. We seldom, if ever, spent our limited funds on frivolous passing fancies.

Neighbors sometimes received free help both in planting and harvesting, if the family had sickness or the man of the family had been victim of an accident and was hurt. People pitched in and planted or harvested his crops for him.

THE FLOWER GARDEN

Growing up was not all cotton and corn. Flowers were cultivated around the yard. The lilac bush outside the kitchen door was my special delight. I basked in the fragrance of the cone shaped blossoms. Even today if I close my eyes, I can imagine the sweet aroma of the dew-covered lilacs on an early spring morning. It was a divine experience.

In the side yard a snowball had huge white balls of blossoms. Next to it grew several delicate pink spireas that I can no longer find at any nursery. Blue altheas grew along the path to the spring. The rambling rose often rambled too far and needed pruning, a sticky job. The lovely red roses were reward enough for any thorn pricks.

Just outside the garden fence stood a row of tall, regal sunflowers. In front of them were hollyhocks, zinnias, marigolds and bachelor buttons. The seeds to annual flowers were carefully gathered and saved for next year. Neighbors sharing seeds gave each family more variety.

SWEET STUFF

We had a small patch of sorghum cane, which had to be cut near the ground. A sharp heavy knife was needed for this. I don't think I ever helped cut it, but I remember lining it up straight on the wagon and going with Dad to the syrup mill. There it was fed into a horse or mule drawn grinder which freed the juice. The juice ran from the grinder into an open cooker. It was cooked down into thick syrup, and put into shiny tin syrup buckets. The owner of the mill kept a portion to pay for the process.

This syrup was used to sweeten fruit, sweet potato pies, and bread puddings, and many other desserts. It made the most delicious candy, and was very tasty on hot biscuits at breakfast. It didn't work as sweetener for cakes, so it was rare for us to have cakes, because cakes needed sugar, and sugar cost money. Cakes were made only on special occasions.

If there was syrup left over to next season it became grainy and was not very good.

SAVING THE GARDEN PRODUCE

Corn was allowed to ripen, that is, become dry on the stalk except for the roastin' ear patch. The roastin' ear patch was a different kind of corn and was for fresh corn on the cob and cut corn for the dinner table. Some was canned for use later. The only method of canning we had was an open kettle. The vegetables were packed in a Mason jar, boiling water was added and the jars sealed with rubber rings and glass tops. They were placed in a large canner kettle, covered with water and allowed to boil for a certain length of time. This method was used for beans, fruits and other vegetables. Some of the food spoiled with this method. Most of it would keep for eating through the winter.

In later years we carried prepared vegetables to the cannery at the county seat in Jasper, where it was put into tin cans like the type you see in the grocery store. I suppose when pressure canners came into use the cannery was no longer needed. I remember it for only a short period of time just before I went away to college.

Another method of food preservation was drying. I have already described drying apples. Green beans were picked and strung whole on a heavy string. The strings were hung up to dry. These were called "leather britches" for obvious reasons. Even though they were soaked in water for some time, they were still tough when cooked and had little flavor. Still, they contained nutrients.

When field peas were allowed to dry on the vine, they were shelled and put into jars to keep the weevils out. However, the weevils sometimes hatched from eggs inside the peas and made them unfit to eat.

Ripe corn was pulled with the dried shuck on it and tossed onto the wagon, driven to the barn and unloaded into the corn-crib. It was stored there and used as needed. Unshucked, it was fed to the animals. When corn meal was needed it was shucked, shelled off the cob and carried to the mill for grinding. Shelling corn from the cob was hard on the hands. If hands were tender, it could result in sore, painful blisters. I heard stories about a "corn shucking", a kind of social at which neighbors got together to shuck corn. If a fellow found a red ear of corn he got to kiss the girl of his choice. I suppose those events went out before my social days.

FIRST TASTES OF SPRING

The first taste of spring was eagerly anticipated. The first harvest of vegetables in the spring was always delicious after eating canned or dried food all winter. One of the first green plants to shoot up in the spring was "poke salat." The tender young leaves had a taste like a cross between spinach and turnip greens. It was boiled in the black iron skillet with fatback.

The leaves were the only part of the plant eaten. The mature plant had lovely purple berries later in summer. We girls liked to crush these and paint our fingernails with the juice, playing grown-up. It stained our fingers along with our nails, which usually were free of color after the first washing. The stain on our fingers remained for several days. We now know the berries, stem and root of this plant is very poisonous. The wild flower book identifies it as Pokeweed.

Other early spring delights were a mess of English Peas (as distinguished from field peas), little spring onions and "grabbled" little new potatoes. Grabbling was the term used to describe the process of obtaining the small potatoes from under the plant without injuring the vines. Mostly it was done by scratching carefully with our fingers into the dirt to uncover and harvest only the ones that were of suitable size to eat. Then we recovered the roots with dirt so the smaller potatoes would continue to grow. The flavor is quite different from cured potatoes. What a delicious meal this was with cornbread and buttermilk.

A row of peanuts might be planted if room was available. Peanuts are a strange plant. The nuts form on the blossom, then turn and bury themselves in the dirt. They are dug, or carefully pulled up, the dirt washed off and then allowed to dry in the sun. The nuts are pulled off the plant and may be allowed to cure for a while before being parched, as we called roasting. We parched them in the shell as are those that are sold at ballparks today. People in many parts of the south consider boiled peanuts a delicacy but in our area peanuts were never boiled.

PREPARING FRUIT AND COMBATING GNATS

We had a couple of apple trees on the place, and they produced pretty well. Dad loved peaches, and several times I remember him planting peach trees. For some reason they never grew and bore fruit. Perhaps our soil was not right for them.

Someone often would come by the house in a truck loaded with baskets of apples, peaches or pears for sale, for perhaps fifty cents a bushel. If Dad had any money at all he would buy at least a peck, and often times a bushel.

What we didn't eat right away we canned. We sat outside to peel them. They seemed to attract gnats that were more annoying than usual. They swarmed in our face and got into our eyes. To combat them we built a fire, and then put sawdust on it so that it would smoke and drive the gnats away. I think it was more punishment for us than the gnats, because it also got into our eyes.

WRINGING THE CHICKEN'S NECK

Preparing a chicken for frying or dumplings was, upon looking back, quite gruesome. However, it was a necessary chore to having meat on the table. One common method of slaughtering was wringing its neck.

The selected bird was taken by the head and slung around in a circle as far as the arm could reach. This succeeded in breaking his neck. Then he would flop around on the ground until he died and was still. At this time his head was cut off so the blood would drain out. If the men in the family happened to be home and not busy they simply chopped off the head eliminating wringing the birds neck. The women didn't quite feel safe with a live flopping chicken and a sharp ax.

The next step was to dip the bird in boiling water. This loosened the feathers so they could be plucked. The odor was very disagreeable. The large feathers were easily removed, but the small pinfeathers were difficult and seemed to take forever. After the chicken was free of feathers, the entrails were removed. Experience taught us to be careful not to pierce them, or we would experience even worse odors. The chicken was then washed and washed and washed. It was cut into parts and salted down until cooking time.

Dad never wanted us to skin the fryers, he said the skin was what made them crisp. Some of us contended that it was the coating of seasoned flour that made them crisp.

Only young tender chickens were used for frying. The "Old Red Rooster" and the old hen needed longer cooking with water to make them tender. They usually ended up being chicken and dumplings.

HOG KILLING TIME

The cool crisp frosty weather of fall brought the sound of leaves crunching underfoot and we knew it was hog killing time. When the weather turned cool, crisp and frosty, the meat would keep and not spoil. Over the past month or so the hog had been fed abundantly to fatten him up for this event. Sometimes a neighbor helped. Then he would receive help in return with this annual chore. The hog usually weighed 75 to 100 pounds, maybe more, and required some muscle power. It was necessary to work swiftly. This job began early in the morning and took all day.

Although we welcomed fresh pork and sausage we also dreaded this day. As children we felt sad because the little pig we had fed and watched grow to be a hog had to become food for the table. On the fateful day we covered our ears with our hands to avoid hearing the rifle shot or the squeal of hog as it was slaughtered.

The hog was then dragged on a sled pulled by one of the mules to the wash place below the spring. The next order of business was scalding with hot water to loosen the hair. Then the hair was meticulously scraped off with knives. I remember helping with this chore. Next the hog was raised with block and tackle to a good working position. He was split from throat to tail and the entrails removed. These were probably taken off and buried.

We never cleaned and stuffed the guts with sausage as some folks did. There was fat around the guts, which was removed, and along with other fat rendered into cracklings and lard. This was done in the iron wash pots. The process was a tricky job, as care had to be taken to keep the fire just so hot not to burn them. The lard was used for baking and frying along with butter. Before margarine and other cooking oils were available this was the only type shortening used.

The cracklings were left after cooking the lard out of the fat. Crisp and tasty bits were used with corn meal to make crackling bread a real country treat.

The meat that was not to be used immediately was packed in layers of salt or brine in the meat box in the smokehouse. The brains, the liver, and souse meat, (from the head of the hog), had to be used or canned. Some of the meat from the head was used to make hogshead jelly. This was more like a spread. Dad and some of the family liked it on biscuits. I never learned to eat these meats. The taste was not pleasing to me and thoughts of the origin were unappealing too.

A major job was sausage making. A good mix of lean to fat went into the sausage. The process was the responsibility of the women. The meat was cut into strips small enough to go into the hand operated meat grinder. The home grown sage and red pepper was added as the meat was ground, being careful not to get the seasoning too concentrated in spots. Whatever sausage was not eaten within a few days had to be canned, however it was never as good as fresh.

When meat was needed for cooking, a trip to the smokehouse was made to procure slices.

JUST NUTS

Frosty fall weather brought ripened black walnuts. There were two large trees in our back yard. The nuts fell to the ground abundantly. The outer shell was soft, mushy and difficult to remove. After stepping on them to crack the outer shell, we used our hands to remove them. The stain on our hands was yellowish brown and took a long time to wear off. We could see why the Indians used these for dye. After the outer shell was removed we lined them up in the sun to dry. People liked the walnuts for making cakes and candy. There was a demand for them, so we were able to sell some to the local store.

The hard inner shell had to be cracked with the hammer on a rock. Then the meats were very difficult to remove. We usually picked out enough meat for candy or a cake, and some just to eat at the time.

We didn't have a hickory tree in the yard, but they were not hard to find in the woods nearby. It was an adventure to go looking for hickory nuts. The outer shell usually came off by itself, although the inner shell is just as hard as walnuts. They have even smaller meats than black walnuts, and are more difficult to pick out of the shell, though not as messy. These nuts have a very different flavor and make the most delicious divinity. A batch of divinity was a special once a year treat for us.

Another nut we went searching for was one we called a chinquapin. They were fairly plentiful at that time. They had a soft shell, easily cracked, and were somewhat like a hazelnut. They were really very tasty. Unfortunately, some blight came along destroying the trees and they no longer can be found.

ROBBING THE BEE HIVES

Robbing the bees was a chore we children didn't particularly relish. No matter what precautions we took this activity always produced a few stings for us. This chore was done after dark, or at dusk, when the bees were most inactive. Our part was to hold the smoke rags so the bees would not swarm out if disturbed. Rags were tied on the end of a stick and set on fire. We did not want them to blaze, just smoke. They were held near the entrance to the hive where the bees entered and left.

Dad had a bee hood that covered his face and shoulders. He removed the cover from over the hive, and took the honey from the top part of the hive. He cut it loose from the sides, and removed layers, leaving enough honey for the bees to feed on through the winter.

He had from five to ten beehives, at different times, and harvested about two quarts per hive. He planted red clover as a source of nectar for the bees. When a new queen was hatched she would take some of the workers, many newly hatched also, and swarm in a cloud outside the hive. Very often they would settle all together on top of each other in a big lump in a tree. It was then when Dad's hood came in very handy as he could capture the swarm and put them in a new hive increasing the number of hives.

Some of the honey was sold, or bartered at the store for other products. Some was kept to eat on hot biscuits for breakfast throughout the winter.

QUILTING

The womenfolk did quilting in the cold winter months. First the quilt top was pieced together in squares of whatever pattern was chosen, tulip leaf, odd patchwork, stars, etc. This was done using scraps of leftover material from dresses, shirts, or garments made throughout the year. Some times neighbors would swap scraps to have more variety in the quilt. The squares were sewn together with borders in between, usually solid unbleached muslin. The quilting frames were put together and hung from the ceiling at a comfortable level for sewing. When not in use they could be rolled up high out of the way.

The backing for the quilt, usually also unbleached muslin, was tacked around the edges of the frame with heavy thread. Next the cotton batting was placed on the backing. Cotton for quilts and pillows was available from spare cotton that was not enough to bale and sell. This cotton batting was hand carded into rolls and unrolled on top of the backing. The quilt top was carefully placed on the batting and tacked at various places to hold it in place. The pattern for the stitches was marked with chalk tied to a string and to the frames in different places to be sure it was evenly quilted.

Now it was ready to quilt. We sat around the quilt trying to keep out of each other's way. This was easy at first, but as the quilting progressed toward the center of the quilt, the frames were rolled up making the work area smaller and smaller.

Each of my sisters had her own favorite needle and we did not dare use another's needle. Some preferred a long slender needle that was easily broken. Others liked a shorter stout needle. As a little girl, I was not allowed to work on a fancy company quilt, because I could not make stitches small and even enough, (I still can't, nevertheless I still quilt) but I was allowed to work on "every day" quilts.

Quilting time was a time for singing, story telling, and later after we acquired one, listening to the radio.

Sometimes the community women made a quilt for a needy family or a new bride. Each woman embroidered her name in the corner of the square she made. They came together for a quilting bee to finish the quilt.

The string quilt was an example of the frugality of the poor people who scratched out a living on family farms in the 1920's and 30's. It was a necessity to make use of every scrap of material, as well as food. The carefully saved scraps were cut into fancy patterns to make beautiful 'company' quilts. These were used when guests spent the night.

Very thin strips were too small to sew together. So, the housewife ingeniously sewed these onto squares of newspaper, or any available paper. The ends were cut off even, the paper peeled off the back and there was a lovely square ready to put together and quilt.

STRING GAMES AND OTHER AMUSEMENTS

We needed adult help with some of the things we did for amusement. Fortunately an older brother or sister seemed to usually be available.

Putting a length of thread through two holes of a button and tying it made a zipper button. Holding an end of the thread around each thumb with the button in the middle, we would spin the button around until the thread became very twisted. Without allowing it to unwind we pulled on each end of the thread and the button would spin round and round twisting and untwisting the thread. At the same time making a noise, which, I suppose, we thought sounded like a zipper. When we continued long enough the thread would wear out and break. However, by this time we were tired of the game and ready to do something else.

Another string trick was making a crow's foot. We looped the circle of string over two hands above the thumbs. By putting the right fingers through, and pulling the thread to the other side and then back, we ended with three toes of string that looked like a crow's foot on each hand. Some people could do many complicated tricks with string.

PAPER DOLLS AND PLAYING HOUSE

Little girls cut paper dolls from the Sears Catalog to play dollhouse. We would cut whole families from the catalog. We cut sofa, tables, beds and chairs from cardboard for them to sit or sleep on. If cut and folded just right they looked pretty nice, espe-
· cially if we could get scraps of material for cushions bedspreads

or decoration. Many happy and busy hours of play were spent with paper dolls and furniture.

Sometimes we played house outside using two rocks with a board across for chairs or tables. We would use broken pieces of dishes for plates. It was such a thrill when one Christmas Santa brought the little tin tea set of which I had been dreaming. It made playing house more fun.

OLD TIRES AND THE ROLLING STORE

Rolling old worn out tires down the hill was a favorite pastime. Our house was at the foot of a steep hill. We would struggle to roll the old tire to the top, then we would race down rolling the tire. Once we got going it was hard to keep up with the tire because it rolled faster than we could run. Then it would roll crooked and run out of the road and into the woods. We could play in the road safely because there was hardly any traffic, mostly just the postman, and the rolling store.

The rolling store could be called an amusement, too, I suppose, since anything out of the ordinary was exciting to us. It came by once a week for some period of time. Available on it was snuff (which most of the older people dipped), flavorings, medicines such as Hadacol and aspirin. Hadacol was a bottled medicine taken for pain. In later years it was revealed to be mostly alcohol. A few canned foods, thread and needles were available, too. I can't remember whether the store took trade goods.

WOODLAND DELIGHTS

The woods on our property were always fascinating to roam. In the spring we delighted in finding sweet shrubs, native azaleas (which we called bush honeysuckle), ginger pitchers and other wild flowers. These, along with dogwood trees were plentiful. When the sweet shrubs were in bloom we tied the fragrant blossoms in our handkerchief and carried them with us anywhere we went to continue to enjoy the scent.

70

A favorite fun activity was climbing to the top of a thin sapling leaning this way and that to get it swinging back and forth, and then swinging all the way to the ground. This provided a thrill that sort of took our breath away, especially if the sapling was tall enough. It had to be a certain kind of tree to bend without breaking, oaks and hickories, I think.

PINE NEEDLE SLEDDING

Though we didn't have much snow we had a sled that Dad had made using old wagon wheel rims for runners, and scraps of lumber for the body.. He also used this to move heavy objects, too small to hitch up the mules for, but too heavy to carry manually.

However we didn't need snow to sled. We made a sled route up the hill behind the hog pen among the thicket of pine trees. By piling the needles on the path and getting a running start, we could pick up speed enough for a good thrilling ride down the steep hill, being careful to miss the trees. Anyone who has tried to walk down a bank covered with pine needles can tell you they are quite slippery.

HOME MADE TOYS

Other toys we needed help with were wooden spool tractors, whistles, and home-carved tops. The tractor was made by cutting series of notches around one end of a wooden spool that thread came on. On the other end a small slot was carved for a short piece of a wooden matchstick to lie in. A rubber band was placed through the middle of a spool around the match piece and another longer matchstick was through the other end of the band. When the stick was turned the band became twisted which caused the tractor to move when placed on the floor.

Another homemade toy was a wooden top. The wooden top had to be carved to balance. Then a heavy string was wound around the top all the way down to the point. When the top was artfully thrown to the floor, right side up, and the end of the string held onto, the unwinding of the string caused the top to spin.

A whistle was made in the spring when the small limbs and bark of the trees were soft and pliable. It took a certain kind of tree sprig about a fourth inch round for the whistle. The bark had to be notched to allow the sound to come out. The bark was slipped off the wood and a slot was cut in the wood to blow into. Then the bark was replaced. We had only two or three holes, but by covering one or the other we could produce a different sound.

FLYING JUNE BUGS

A favorite amusement that we enjoyed in the summer was flying June bugs. The only material we needed for this activity was a piece of string and a large bug that had a shiny iridescent green back. They were plentiful around the first to last of June, and catching them was easy. We tied the string to the bug's leg, which took two of us, one to hold it and one to tie, because no bug is going to sit still and be tied up. Then we let the bug go, but he could fly only to the end of the string. His wings made a pleasant buzzing sound as he flew round and round. When we tired of him we released him. Sometimes he would try so hard to get loose he would lose his leg. We had no regret, always figuring he would make a good meal for a bird.

MAYPOP PEOPLE

A vine we called apricot grew vigorously on our place. Now I know it is a maypop. It had a lovely blue aster like flower that later formed a green bulb. We put two of these together with a stick. We put stick arms and legs on them and could even make eyes and mouth by scraping the green off with a sharp stick. We made whole families of these maypops—mamas, daddies, children and babies.

READING

As far back as I can remember we all enjoyed reading. Before I could read for myself, Mama, an older brother or sister read the funny papers to me. Barney Google, Lil' Abner, Dagwood Bumstead, and the Katzenjammer Kids were some of our favorites. Not all of cartoon strips were funny. We could hardly wait for the next Dick Tracy or Brenda Starr episode to see if they escaped the bad people who were threatening them.

We had a Bible storybook that we enjoyed as children. It had many lovely pictures in it. I remember the big family Bible as being too heavy for me to lift as a child. In it were recorded birthdays and deaths On Sunday morning my Dad always spent some time reading the Bible. Sunday was a day of rest from much of the work we did. Of course there were chores which could not wait, such as the milking, cooking, etc., but we didn't work in the fields and had time to spend as we pleased.

Over a period of time my brother collected Zane Gray's books, which probably came to include all this author's work. These were typical "Cowboy and Indian" novels of massacres, bloody and full of trouble. They stimulated our imagination and we loved them. The ending was not always good, but with so little material to read, we avidly read and reread them.

When my sister, Grace started high school we had access to the school library, and the county library which was close enough to the school for her to use. When she checked out a book the whole family wanted to read it, but she couldn't keep it that long. We came up with the idea of reading aloud each night. We finished our homework early, so that when we finished cleaning the kitchen after supper we could all gather around to listen. We took turns reading. Dad was one of the most enthusiastic of the group. We enjoyed it so much we were reluctant to blow out the light and go to bed, when the time came.

Among the books we read were Robert Louis Stevenson's *Treasure Island*, Mark Twain's novels and many other classics.

THE LOFT

I suppose the loft could be classified as an amusement, for the children at least. The loft (or attic) in our house consisted of a small hole in the ceiling fitted with a cover, which was pushed aside to enter. To get into the loft we had to climb on a chair, push the cover off, grasp the edge of the ceiling and pull ourselves up. It was only after we grew to be pretty big kids that we were able to perform this feat. There was a separate loft above the front porch.

The loft was a general storage area for all and everything we wanted out of the way, or the grown-ups wanted to hide from the children. Thus it was a source of fascination for us. I particularly remember sneaking up there to read my older sister's True Story magazines that someone had given her. In those days this magazine was considered as bad as pornography, and too racy reading for young girls; however they were much milder than the regular novels of today.

When my brother Ken and I were big enough to climb into the loft, we played a joke on our little brother Sam. We were finding interesting things to bring down. When Sam asked about them, we told him there was a good snake in the loft that was giving them to us. Later we heard Sam saying, "Oh, Lord help me get up into the loft." We still tease him about it.

PINE ROSIN GUM

Chewing gum was not a necessary item to purchase consequently we seldom had any. As a substitute we looked for pine trees that had a cut or crack and had oozed pine "rawzen." When it became somewhat thick, it chewed almost as well as gum, but the flavor left something to be desired.

MEDICINE

Some of the medicines I remember having on hand were castor oil and Black Draught for constipation or just when someone didn't feel well generally. Hadacol or Geritol bought from the rolling store was supposed to cure headaches. Musterole and Vicks Salve were rubbed on the chest for croup, or congestion as it is called now. Sometimes these were put on a flannel cloth on the chest or back. Occasionally turpentine was used on the cloth, but could burn the skin if too much was used. Peroxide, merthiolate and iodine were used for cuts and scratches or skin infections.

Every year in the spring the children were given a teaspoon of sugar with a few drops of turpentine. I don't remember precisely what this was for, but I think it was to purge us of any worms we might have picked up in our digestive system. The taste was so bad even the sugar couldn't cover it up.

Paregoric, which today is a prescription drug, was available then. It was used as a last resort to help a crying baby sleep and just a drop or two worked wonders.

In those days doctor's made house calls, however, in the rural areas a doctor was sent for only when a person was deathly ill, or to confirm an illness suspected to be "catching" such as measles.

My younger brother had a stomachache and fever, which would not go away. Doc Turk came and diagnosed appendicitis. He went to the hospital for surgery. The whole family was very worried about him. A niece had died when the diagnosis was not made early enough. An appendectomy was not the routine surgery that it is today.

The birth of a baby required the doctor's services. All the women in our part of the country delivered their babies at home. They had no prenatal care unless they had serious symptoms of trouble.

Children were not as knowledgeable then as now. Babies, pregnancy, and especially sex were "hush-hush" subjects. I can faintly remember when my younger brother was born. It was the day after Christmas. Night was falling but it was still somewhat light out. I was bundled up and sent to my brother's house over the hill. I can remember my older sister bathing Mama's face as I prepared to leave. I knew the doctor had been sent for but I was not aware of what was happening. When I came home next day I had a new baby brother.

"Doc Turk" was what we called our doctor. I remember no other name. He had a gruff bedside manner and we were quite scared of him. He lived in Nelson, a town about three or four miles away. The only time he was called to see me was to confirm a bad case of the "red" measles. My brother Ken and I were exposed at school and were both pretty sick. I was in the seventh grade and Ken was in the fourth.

No one in the family had had measles except Dad. The measles were feared for adults because they could bring serious complications. No sooner had Ken and I begun to recover than the other family members began to "take sick." Soon one or two people with measles, including Mama occupied every bed in the house. It was like a hospital ward. There was Lenora, Thenia, Grace, Oveda, Herschel, Sam, Sherman, and Mama, all sick at the same time.

Since it was very cold Ken and I were told to stay inside for fear of a relapse. We were kept busy waiting on the sick ones. We particularly had to watch my oldest sister. She had such a high fever she didn't know what she was doing and would get out of bed barefoot saying she had to go milk the cows. Dad had to take care of all the outdoor chores like milking, feeding the animals, water and wood. A neighbor woman came in to do the cooking and washing for the duration.

Clora and Herbert were married and away from home at the time. Clora, who had married a second time, was exposed to the measles and pregnant with her first child. It could affect the child adversely. To try to create immunity in her, Doc Turk took a small amount of blood from my arm and injected it into hers. I suppose it worked. She either had a very mild case or none, because there were no complications with her pregnancy.

Before I leave the subject of medicine I must tell a story that stands out in my memory. When we were small and misbehaved we were often threatened with a dose of the castor oil, which we hated more than a switching because of the awful taste. I don't remember the threat ever being carried out, but once my oldest sister tried to give me some as punishment.

In a large family the older children had to assume responsibility for the younger ones. The youngsters learned to respect and obey this sibling almost as they would the mother. In our family this was Lenora. I must have been almost teen age, sort of feisty, sassy and rebellious, when the incident happened. I can't even remember what I had done. Lenora was determined to give me Castor Oil, and I was just as determined not to take it. I remember thinking it was not a proper punishment. We struggled and she had me down in the floor. She held my nose so I would have to open my mouth. I wiggled and squirmed until the Castor Oil spilled on the floor. Finally she decided to give up. Mama and my other sisters were watching but didn't interfere. I can imagine them trying to keep from giggling.

FRIENDS

We had friends at school but my two next older sisters and I probably liked the friends who lived about two miles away by road but about one half mile if we went through the woods. They had three girls about our ages. We liked to just walk and talk or play some kind of games on Sunday afternoon, or sometimes we would sing together. When we visited each other our Mamas would tell us we could stay an hour, or perhaps an hour and a half. When we arrived we would ask a grown up to tell us when the time was up. We wanted to be home on time so our Mama would not worry, and to stay in her good graces for the next time we asked to go visit.

One summer I spent several weeks with my sister Clora, when she was feeling "poorly", to help her take care of the babies, and do other chores. I felt really grown up, but I had a long way to go. I was probably in the seventh grade, or about twelve years old.

My best friend Thelma lived within sight of Clora's house and we got together to play as often as we could. She had chores to do, also, so we made a hole in the bank of the road about half way between the houses that we called our mailbox. We wrote notes two or three times a day and carried them to the "box," collecting them when we were free to run up there. I don't remember what we wrote about. It was just a silly secret thing young people think up to do at this age. We probably asked when the other could get together to play, what the other was doing that morning and perhaps about a boy we might like. I was a year older than Thelma, so when we started high school we were in a different class and sort of drifted apart and both had other best friends.

COUNTRY LANGUAGE

Country people have a special language all their own, and this differs from area to area. All dialects and pronunciations are quite unique from the mountains of north Georgia to middle and South Georgia. For example where I grew up we made an extra effort to pronounce the letter "r," even to the point of emphasizing them. We slept on "pillars" and opened "winders." We put an "r" in words where there was none. "Ort" was used for ought, for example, "You ort to wash your hands."

The plantation south dialect abhors the "r." My husband, who grew up in middle Georgia, never pronounces an "r" except when the word begins with an "r." He says "wuh" for were, "nevah" for never.

Southerners put two or three syllables in one-syllable words. We like to stretch words out, for example; "Go to the sto-er (store) and get some flou-er (flour)."

As a greeting when a car passed by (or wagon), men would "throw up their hand." Men never waved to each other. It was not manly. Only women waved. A typical question might be, "Who was that passed by in the car?" Answer, "I don't know but he must a knowed me, he throwed up his hand."

If some one had lost weight the remark was, "He sure has fallen away."

"Light n'stay a while" meant have a seat and visit. Apparently this saying came from noting how a butterfly flits from one flower to the next never alighting on one for long.

"Light out" meant leave. "Lit," was used as past tense for light. "He just lit out like he seen a ghost" meant he left in a hurry. The expression could be used about a person or an animal.

"The dog lit out like his tail was on fire." Sometimes when the day was over and the mules tired and hungry they would "light out" for home.

If some one was pale it could be said, "He looks plum puny." Sometimes we might be "Out of sorts" or depressed and ornery, then we were said to "have the mulligrubs."

When asked, "How are you?" the answer might be "just common." I suppose this meant no better and no worse than usual.

Old timers used "holp" as past tense of help. "I holp him fix the wagon." Past tense was used often this way.

When we had a hard time getting up a bank, a hill or over a fence, we would "take a run and go." At times the road was slick with rain and the car wheels would spin and the car stall on the hill. Then dad would back down the hill and "take a run and go."

A paper sack was a "poke." "Whatcha got in that poke?" Some people "toted their lunch in a poke."

"I'm fixing to" meant "I'm getting ready to do—so and so." It might be used in leaving for school, the store or work; as "I'm fixing to milk the cow."

The word "scrouge" meant very close together. "Maybe I can scrouge one more biscuit in the lunch bucket." Or "too many people were sitting on the bench and I was scourged up so tight against the side I could hardly breathe."

"Shorts" was something we fed the hogs a bucket of.

"Drekly" was another widely used expression. It meant in a little while. "I'll be by your house drekly," meant I would be there soon.

Sometimes when Dad had to stop the wagon or car on a hill we would "scotch" it. That is, we found a large rock to put in front of the wheels. This was extra protection to keep it from rolling in case the brakes did not hold.

"Founder" meant eating so much it made the person or animal sick. "You're eating enough to founder yourself."

Another oft heard phrase when seeing a child for the first time in a while might be, "The last time I saw you, you were knee high to a duck." Or "I've known him since he was knee high to a duck."

When asked, "What did you say?" a man might reply, "I don't chaw my tobaccer but once."

If we were misbehaving we might hear this threat, "I'll get a hickory and wear you out." A hickory is a switch cut from a hickory tree.

After a hard day's work, people said, "I'm plum wore out."

A shady character was as slick as wet soap.

"There ain't nothing to him," meant he was totally worthless.

If someone was overly proud of himself he had "the big head."

"He don't know gee from haw," was a slow person who was not bright.

Different dialects make for interesting conversation and are pleasing to listen to. With the event of TV much of our language differences are being lost or amalgamated into one. Here is hoping it never disappears because it defines a people.

THAT OLD TIME RELIGION

Religion was a large part of life growing up on the farm. As early as I can remember, Dad cleaned out the wagon, hitched up the mules and off we went to "the meeting house." There was only one seat in the wagon. It was high and had springs. Dad sat there to drive the mules, and usually Mama and an older sister or brother sat beside him. We considered a turn on the seat a great treat. Most of the time we put quilts down to sit on and rode with our feet hanging off the back of the wagon bed to the meeting house. We dressed in our Sunday best. We only had one new Sunday dress each year. We out grew them quite fast so it was considered a waste to have more.

A community was often called by the church's name; thus when we moved to Pickens County we lived in Four Mile Community about a half mile from the Four Mile Creek in one direction and a half mile from Four Mile Creek Baptist Church in the other direction. Today there is a sign at the turn from the main road saying, "Four Mile Church, two miles." This sign was featured on a national television program as an oddity. I suppose they wanted to show what hicks country people were. No one told them the church was named for the creek, which was four miles long and not the distance to the church.

While living here, we walked to church. Four Mile Church was the church where we were members. There were churches in many nearby communities. Most of the country churches had meeting once a month. Oprah had the first Sunday, Yellow Creek second, ours was the third and Corinth was fourth. Many people would visit other churches if the weather and transportation allowed.

Each Saturday before meeting day was conference day. This was a business meeting with minutes and reports. I don't remember much about it, probably because I was small and uninterested in what was going on. There was a short service afterward.

The Sunday service was sometimes quite long. If there were visiting preachers they were asked to take part, and often there were several. The preaching was "fire and brimstone," very emotional. Sinners were asked to come to the front mourners' bench to be prayed over, to repent their sins and be saved. Some of the older women might "get happy" and shout "Hallelujah, praise the Lord" along with some preachers. I never saw my mother do this. She was quiet, almost shy, and never demonstrated her emotions. I learned only recently that she belonged to the Methodist Church before she married Dad.

My father was a preacher, called by God, ordained by the Southern Baptist, and was in the middle of all church activities. He did not serve as pastor of a church, but helped conduct revivals and spoke as a visiting preacher at other churches in the area. I remember him reading the big family Bible every Sunday morning early. He always asked a blessing before meals. If a guest minister was "setting down" with us for dinner, he was asked to say the blessing. When Dad wasn't there we had no blessing because it was not considered proper, I suppose, for the girls to pray aloud.

In August we had a week of "protracted" or revival meetings when we met twice a day, once at eleven a.m. and again at night.

A visiting preacher was invited to conduct these meetings and sometimes a special song leader from some other church was invited also. A special offering was taken at the end of the week to give both. Many people came who sang at other churches and were asked to join the singers at the organ.

The Sunday morning following the revival was "the baptizing." (It was always called "the baptizing." People would ask "Are you going to the baptizing at Corinth next Sunday?") All the sinners who had been saved and joined the church lined up at the cement baptizing pond. The preacher took them one at a time and put them under the water briefly, while the people watched. They wore regular clothes but removed their shoes. Then they had to go home and change or bring dry clothing with them to change before the closing service. I was eleven years and eight months when I was baptized.

Some churches had a creek or branch they dammed up for the baptism. Four Mile church had an above ground cement pool, filled by diverting water from a small stream. It was in a shady place it the woods nearby. The next week after the baptizing the children all wanted to go swimming in the baptizing pool. Most couldn't really swim but it was cool and we had a good time nonetheless. This lasted until the pool became dirty and filled with falling leaves. Then it had to be drained.

There was a service in spring that we called "The May Meeting." It was also the once a year communion service. All the churches around had these services, and people visited as many as they could. It was an "all day meeting with dinner on the ground." It began with singing and preaching. Next everyone was dismissed to go outside for the dinner. Every family brought their best cooking and it was a feast.

After dinner the singers would start and it would be time to cover the food and go back inside. The afternoon session was communion and then foot washing. The scripture pertaining to these rituals was read at the appropriate time.

It was mostly the older people who participated in these rituals. Perhaps the young were shy, or perhaps it was thought that the right to participate was earned with years. The people who participated took communion. Then they removed their shoes for the foot washing. A long towel was tied around the waist and the basin filled with water. The women washed each other's feet in a basin and dried them and men washed men's feet. This was an emotional experience, and some times resulted in much shouting. One woman I particularly remember always "got happy", as the person's state was called. She would dance up and down in the aisle clapping her hands and shout "Hallelujah, Praise God." This service seemed to make people feel cleansed and renewed in the spirit.

Most of the young people could get away with staying outside visiting and talking during the afternoon. The girls thought they had to have a new dress for the "May Meeting." It was the beginning of spring with new growth on flowers and trees budding out. With nature wearing her new clothes we wanted something new to wear. We picked spring-like fabrics such as thin voiles and dotted Swiss Invariably the weather hit a cool spell and we shivered but wore the dress proudly anyway. I don't remember what the fellows wore. This day was a social occasion and the girls could possibly meet a fellow. If they were lucky he might ask to walk them home. A lot of courting went on after church, both at May meeting and revivals.

FUNERALS

A death in the community was just another part of life, and an extension of the church service. When a death occurred the body was brought home from the funeral home to lie-in-state in the living room. Neighbors would come by to pay their respects and bring food. They would also take turns "setting up with the dead" and various people would be there all night.

The casket would then be taken to the church in the hearse, carried up the steps by the pallbearers, and opened for the service. Several preachers took part and many sad songs were sung. It was sometimes a very long service. Then the congregation filed by the casket to take a last look. All the people knew each other in the neighborhood and attended with their children. Children were not shielded from the natural world.

When I was a very small child I think people were expected to moan and cry profusely at a loved one's funeral. This was a sign that they really loved the dearly departed. If they did not feel like crying already, the sad songs and impassioned sermons of the preachers would bring on the tears.

The casket was closed and transported to the church cemetery by the pallbearers where it was lowered into a grave that had been dug by caring friends. The friends proceeded to shovel the dirt into the grave to cover the casket and fill the grave. Flowers would then be put on and around the grave.

When I was young, flowers from the florist were rarely seen. Perhaps in the dead of winter some might be used. Mostly people made sprays of flowers from their yards and brought them. A close loved one would usually pinch off one particularly pretty flower to carry home and to dry in the Bible as a remembrance.

The cemetery had no hired caretakers. Each family kept their plot clean. There were plots whose family had died out or moved away. To clean these the church had a special Decoration Day. Every able bodied person in the community showed up with hoes, rakes and whatever tools were needed to clean the cemetery. It was a workday but people were able to catch up on the news of the area.

A DIFFERENT ERA

My father had always been a staunch Republican and was contemptuous of people getting "something for nothing." The Roosevelt era and New Deal was to make a great change in our lives.

As part of the New Deal the Civilian Conservation Corp was formed to create jobs. When my oldest brother Herschel joined the CCC, Dad lost his best plow hand. Herbert had been married at sixteen and was farming for his own growing family. Kenneth would have been about ten years old and could not replace a grown son in the field, even though he tried.

The CCC unit to which Herschel belonged helped to build state parks all over Georgia that are enjoyed even today. On the heels of this came World War II. Herschel was in his twenties, single, and a prime draft subject. The war would change our lives and the lives of many people forever.

Shortly before the war we managed to acquire a radio. The radio opened a whole new world of entertainment to rural families. The tubes, which looked like an elongated light bulb, burned out and had to be replaced often. The radio was powered by a large battery that we carefully rationed for fear it would give out and we might not have the funds to replace it. There was much static and crackling and often the station drifted away and could not be heard. It always occurred at a very exiting moment in the mystery of which we were engrossed.

We liked to listen to scary things like *The Hounds of the Baskerville.* Some favorites were *George Burns and Gracie Allen, The Lone Ranger, Amos and Andy,* and *I Love a Mystery.* Mama and my older sisters tried to plan work so as not to miss the afternoon soaps, *One Man's Family,* and *Our Miss Brooks.* They were called soaps because they were sponsored by the soap companies and aimed at the female audience who usually had the choice of what soap was used. We all stayed up as late on Saturday night as Dad would allow, listening to the *Grand Ole Opry.* We loved Uncle Dave Macon a banjo player, and Minnie Pearl a comedian, and also the other singing stars.

People were caught up in the story on radio much more than on television today, because they had to use their imagination. Often we were really scared, and on the edge of our chair. Sudden noises would make us jump and the howls of an animal would make our hair almost stand on edge. Often we'd be so charged up we couldn't go to sleep. We didn't dare tell or complain, however, because we might not be allowed to listen next time.

In addition to his Sunday Bible studies, Dad listened to gospel singing on Sunday morning. Thus it happened that our radio was on, and we caught the first announcement on that infamous day of December 7, 1941 when the Japanese attacked Pearl

Harbor. This was my first year in high school and just before my 14th birthday. We could not have imagined what an enormous effect it would have on our lives.

PICKENS COUNTY HIGH SCHOOL

The school bus had started running a few years before to transport rural children to high school. When it rained we had to walk about a mile and a half, because the bus couldn't negotiate the slick roads of red mud without slipping, sliding and sometimes getting stuck in the ditch.

Grace, Oveda and I were attending Pickens County High at Jasper, which was about ten miles from home. Several schools had been consolidated from the small towns in the county. It was strange to me to be in a large school with a lot of people we didn't know.

It's odd the sort of things one remembers. A part of my initiation for Beta Club membership was getting the autograph of all the teachers on a raw egg without breaking it. The physical education teacher Mr. McMillan put a crack in mine, but it didn't leak. Some people had fun trying to break another person's egg.

I recall vividly all the classes lining up for immunization shots. The county nurse and doctor came to the gym and set up the equipment. The classes were called one at a time. We had a series of three typhoid shots a week apart, and then smallpox. It really did not hurt so much but a lot of people fainted just at the thought of it. Most of us had never seen a doctor before and were scared. Our arms were sore for a long time, and the boy's thought it jolly sport to come by and punch our sore arm. The polio and measles vaccine had not been developed then.

For physical education class we were required to have a gym suit. It was a one-piece outfit with short sleeves and bloomer type legs having elastic above the knees. We had never been allowed to wear shorts, and were only allowed to wear long pants to work in the fields. Dad didn't think it right for girls to show a lot of bare legs. He agreed to allow the gym suits since girls had gym classes separate from boys and changed right there in the gym, without going outside.

We had no football at our small schools but we had both girls and boys basketball.

Grace graduated that year, the spring of '42. She borrowed $10.00 and went to board in Marietta to attend the National Youth Administration training. Dad was very pessimistic declaring that she would never be able to repay the money. He did not believe in borrowing money and considered it somewhat of a disgrace to owe money. However, Grace was a stubborn, determined kind of girl who went on with her plans.

The National Youth Administration was a school connected with Roosevelt's defense program. Grace learned radio technology and then was employed at the Bomber Plant, the name by which the Bell Aircraft Corporation was commonly called. She installed the radios in the B-17 bombers, called the Flying Fortress, that were vital to the war.

Needless to say she was able to pay back the $10.00 plus saving enough to attend Reinhardt College and earn her teacher's certificate. As the first in the family to finish high school and go to college, she graduated with top honors and was valedictorian of her class. Grace was an inspiration and help to the younger ones in the family.

TATE HIGH SCHOOL

The Sam Tate family had founded the Tate Marble Company at Marble Hill and Tate, Georgia. He and his family had built a lovely pink marble mansion, where they lived. It has now been converted into a noted restaurant, museum and bed and breakfast place. The Tates had also built a white marble school, which they maintained for their employees' children. By the time for my second year in high school the Tates had sold the Tate Marble Company to Georgia Marble, and the private school became public. We had envied the children who could attend the beautiful school made of white marble and were delighted to spend the remainder of our high school days there. One advantage it afforded was that it was about half the distance of Pickens High and therefore a shorter bus ride.

I was thrilled to be accepted as a member of the high school glee club. The club sang for chapel programs and special events. We had a recital each year. We often acted out the music. I especially remember *The Old Lamp Lighter* and *Surrey with the Fringe on Top*, which we did with action and props.

During my school years we had chapel once a week. Our piano teacher played a rousing march as the classes came into the auditorium. We always pledged allegiance to the flag, sang the national anthem and state song. We had devotion with Bible reading, a prayer, and sometimes a poem. Classes and school groups presented skits, debates, and other types of programs. When there was no special program we sang patriotic songs or classic songs from a school songbook. We loved the chapel singing. Today's children really are missing out on something special.

THE WAR YEARS

These years were quite traumatic for our family as well as many others around us. Most families had sons who were drafted and serving in some branch of the military. We had two from our family.

Herschel was at first deferred because of his eyesight and Herbert because of his family. As the war continued and more men were needed they were both moved up from the classification of 4-F status to 1-A, and called up at different times.

Herschel served parade duty in Washington D.C. in the Air Force. He said people thought it was easy duty, but standing for hours in all kind of weather waiting for the parade to start was no picnic. Every button, and buckle had to shine like new pennies, shoes had to be shined and uniforms had to be clean and perfectly free of wrinkles.

Later the parades for every visiting dignitary were discontinued and Herschel was given other duty. He became a cook and was stationed with the command in Burma and India. He contracted malaria, which bothered him the rest of his life.

Herbert was in the infantry. He served in the foxholes during the allied crossing of the Rhine River in Germany. He has never wanted to talk about his wartime experiences. They must have been pretty grim. He did tell a few funny stories that happened. He lost much of his hearing when a shell exploded too close and received a medical discharge and a Purple Heart.

Nell and Herbert lived in a four-room house just over a steep hill from us. While he was away in service I spent my nights with Nell and the children, so they would not be alone. I would get off the bus at home, see what the news was, whether we had received a letter from either brother, what I needed to do or take. Then I would walk up and over the hill to their house. I can remember times when it was so cold my lungs would be aching from breathing the cold air as I hurriedly climbed the steep hill and went down the other side. The trail was partly beside a field and partly through a wooded pasture. If I had gone the road it would have been twice as far.

Mama remained practically glued to the radio during news time, hoping to hear good news of the war that would allow her sons to return home safely. I can imagine how she worried about them.

School was geared to the war effort. We sang patriotic songs with fervor at our chapel program every week. We all hoarded our pennies to buy saving stamps. On the radio and at school we heard and sang war songs. Boosting the sale of war bonds was *Any Bonds Today*? performed by the most famous singers and actors of the day. War bonds sold at $18.50 and would mature at $25.00. There were $50 bonds and higher priced bonds. Children bought war stamps at 10 and 25 cents each, pasted them in a book and hoped to eventually have enough to trade for a bond.

Other songs were: "One and one makes two you see, Two and two make four. You and you can win this war, these figures indicate. For it's not the large amount: it's the little things that count, (mend those shoes. Bits of meat make tasty stews,) etc."

There were derogatory songs about the Nazi, Fascist and Japanese leaders. "There's a big fat hog over in Rome. He'd have been better off if he'd stayed home, but he kept right on rooting on the other fellow's land, 'til he rooted right into Hitler's hand, etc" The one about Japan ended, "and the sun that is rising will go down on that day," referring to the sun on the Japanese flag.

The home front was a very strong part of the war effort that demonstrated the patriotic zeal of people of all ages. Posters were put up in all public places, urging people to plant victory gardens and to save in every way possible so that more supplies could be sent to the troops. Also the famous "UNCLE SAM WANTS YOU" poster came to be most familiar to everyone.

The girls in all home economics classes were required to take a Red Cross course in first aid. We learned how to make hospital beds, make splints, and bathe and care for patients. The government had not ruled out that America might be bombed, and everyone needed to be prepared. In the big cities and near military posts there were bomb shelters. It was thought that rural areas would not be a target for attack.

When our nurse was teaching us how to bathe a patient she said, "You start at the head, bathing down as far as possible. Then start at the feet and bathe up as far as possible. Last you bathe 'possible.'" We spent our free periods at school and study hall rolling bandages for the Red Cross.

Many girls sat with groups of friends out on the bank of the road in front of the school during lunch breaks just chatting and enjoying the fresh air. Sometimes a convoy of soldiers would pass with the young men greeting us and tossing out names and addresses that the girls scurried to collect. After all, it was our patriotic duty to write any serviceman who was away from home and needed mail to ward off loneliness. After all, stamps were only 3 cents. Pen pals were encouraged and some led to lasting love and lifetime commitments.

At home we scoured the premises for scrap iron, old nails, old horseshoes, pieces of wagon wheel rims, and such, to help with the building of war machinery. A truck came by to collect whatever we had found. I think we were paid a few cents for it. That was probably our source of money for savings stamps.

Then there was rationing. The government issued a book of stamps for each family. A stamp allowed the family to buy a certain amount, each week or month, of the goods that were rationed. When the rationed item was bought a stamp was turned in and when the stamps were all spent you could buy no more of the item until next month. The items I remember most were sugar, gas and coffee. There must have been other things that were rationed, which were scarce due to the war and high priority to the troops. We probably never used all our allotment since we were not accustomed to using a lot of sugar, and we didn't travel much either so we didn't need much gas. I heard of people selling their stamps to others, but no one we knew would be so unpatriotic as to buy or trade rationing stamps on the black market.

We had an old green Chevy car at that time. It would never start. I suppose the battery was dead or very nearly so. When we needed to go somewhere we had to get out and push the car off down the hill and get it going fast enough to make the motor start. I suppose we were lucky to live on a hill.

In order to save on gas the driver would cut off the motor and allow the car to coast down the hill, and then he would cut it on just as we came to the bottom of the hill. This would not be possible in today's automatic automobiles. We used the car to pick up our brothers at the bus or take them back when they were on furlough.

This is the only car I remember. My brother told me stories of an old Model-T that they once owned. It seems Dad was an atrocious driver and quite often wound up in the ditch. Then someone had to take the mules and pull him out. According to the stories he took a lot of kidding about getting into the moonshine and ending up in the ditch.

Many soldiers on leave hitchhiked home and back to camp. Nobody ever passed a soldier without stopping to pick him up. He could be going home on furlough prior to being sent overseas, and surely if it were our brother we'd want someone to give him a ride. During the war soldiers were required to wear their uniform at all times.

When the war was over many soldiers returned to marry their sweethearts. Herschel married Lucille while on furlough shortly before the war ended. Oveda, who had been attending North Georgia College studying to be a teacher, married Harold shortly after he returned home.

In May of '45, just as I was finishing high school, Germany surrendered, followed by Japan on September 2.

It was customary for the senior class to take a trip, usually to Washington D.C. Gas and travel were still restricted, making it necessary for my class to curtail travel. As young people do, they felt deprived and prevailed upon the principal to allow them a short trip. The group spent a week at a 4-H camp near by, preparing our own food, singing camp songs, hiking and swimming in the pool. All high school girls had autograph books and this gave us plenty of time to finish getting classmates autographs and any little verse they wanted to add. I recently found mine in an old trunk at my sister's. Remembering each person who wrote there is not easy.

By this time I was 17 years old and preparing to go away to school. My grades were very good, near the top of the class. My principal encouraged me to attend college. He gave me information about Berry College, a school where I could work for my tuition, room and board. He was instrumental in my acceptance and enrollment there.

My experiences at Berry College are a whole other episode in the story of my life.

ORIGINAL POEMS
by Lois Stewart

THE BATTLE

Spring is sprung
The weeds are growing.
I must get out
And do some hoeing.

All kinds of vines
Are covering our fence.
And against them
I've very little defense.

I fight them fiercely
With shears and hoe.
But they continue
To flourish and grow.

I must confess
I hate to begin.
I'm firmly convinced
The vines will win.

DANDELION

O dandelion of yellow,
How very lovely you look,
As you cluster along the roadside
In every cranny and nook.

But make your home in a lawn,
You'll be uprooted come dawn.
I've heard that you are edible,
And think it quite incredible!!

DEEP CREEK

Clear, sparkling mountain stream
Flowing, flowing free,
Ever going forward
To your meeting with the sea.

Pure, cool rippling waters
Spilling over rocks and sand,
Trilling a soft lullaby
To all who understand.

Swiftly rushing waters
Sending up misty spray,
Gushing over waterfalls
That appear along your way.

Chrystal shimmering pools
Glistening in the sun,
Reflecting lovely sunsets
At dusk, when day is done.

Cold, crisp mountain stream
Over hung with shade,
Nipping, nipping, chilling toes
Of those who dare to wade.

Soft refreshing water
Spinning tubers round,
Whirling, twirling downstream
With native, soothing sound.

JESUS MEANS

Jesus means that I need never fear,
For He is always near,
If I am lonely,
He, too, has felt loneliness.
If I feel rejected,
He has walked that path before me.
If I suffer pain,
He has suffered more.
When I am dying,
He has experienced that with dignity.
Wherever I go,
He has been.
Whatever I feel,
He has felt.
He walks beside me in all life has dealt.
And I need never fear.

NO HARP FOR ME

Dear Lord when Gabriel blows his blast
And I come home to rest at last
Don't measure me for harp and wings
Let me have instead these things:
A garden spot with soft rich soil
Some garden tools with which to toil
Give me plants and plenty of seeds
But please, God, omit the weeds.
Water my plot with soft cool rain
Then let the sun come out again.
And when the flowers bloom in spring
Give me butterflies on the wing.
I would like a bench to sit upon
To watch the birds and hear their song.
Give me permission to sometimes crow
About the roses that I grow.

SOUTHERN COOKIN'

O that southern cookin'
The goodest in the land,
Northern folks miss sompin.
Their taste buds must be bland.

No recipe is needed.
Jist cook like Mamma, please.
Fill the great big iron pot
With fresh shelled field peas.

Add a chunk a boilin' meat
N'get the fire a goin',
In the ol wood burnin' stove
Til the flame's a glowin'.

Shove in som' scrubbed sweet taters.
They're yummy soft n' hot.
With gobs o' fresh-churned butter
They really hit the spot.

Let's grabble new Irish taters.
Pick us a mess a beans,
Bake us up a cornpone,
N' fry some streak-o-lean.

A tasty dish of turnip greens
Southerners view with zeal.
But to our northern neghbors
Greens have no "taste appeal."

Ham n' eggs jist ain't the same
Without our country grits.
Northern folks turn noses up,
They think we've lost our wits.

"Y'all cum to see us",
Our drawl has southern charm.
The clipped accent o'northern folk
Somehow seems not as warm.

Although our worlds are closer,
N' oft the twain do meet,
O pray preserve our southern ways
Else our country's incomplete.

Luther B. Wehunt
Lois Wehunt
Frances Everet Wehunt

All Eleven
Sherman, Sam, Kenneth,
Lois, Oveda, Grace,
Herbert, Herschel,
Thenia, Clora, Lenora

Home Place near Four Mile Church
Grace, Mama, Ken, Booty, Sam

Luther, Lenora, Lois, Sam, Grace
Kenneth, Oveda
Frances Everet, Granny Winkler

Sisters
Grace, Lois, Oveda

Nell, Herbert
Ralph, Mildred, Doris, Baby Frances

Herschel and Lucille

Henry or Kate

Lois and Grace
Rub-a-dub-dub
one pup in a tub

Barn door on Wehunt farm

Wagon on Wehunt farm

Clora Wehunt, Luther Wehunt
Lenora Wehunt, Frances Wehunt

Arthur Wehunt, Luther Wehunt
Barney Strickland, Leatha Wehunt Strickland,
Frances Everet Wehunt

Great Grandmother (maternal)
Frances Carver Worley

Frances Everet (mama)
Parthenia Worley Winkler (grannie)
Addie Worley (aunt) and Little Lois

Lois Wehunt at HS graduation

**Scene at Old Federal school
Kenneth is 2nd row left**

High School graduation picture
Lois is front row, 3rd from left

Miles Allen Winkler, Lois' grandfather

William Martin Wehunt, grandfather

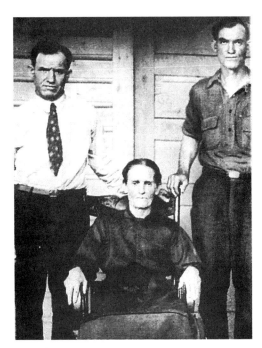

Carl Winkler, Elmer Winkler
Pathenia Worley Winkler (grandmother)

Rebecca Roper Wehunt, grandmother

113

Sign at Hwy 5 and Four Mile Church road

Henry, one of our mules

About the Author

Lois Wehunt grew up in the mountains of north Georgia on a small farm in Pickens County during the depression years. She was one of eleven children, with five brothers and five sisters. She was the fourth from the youngest and was youngest girl. Her parents never made much money, but there was always enough to get by on. There was plenty of love and companionship, fun and games, along with lots of hard work. Country life was very different from big city life, and they had to "make do" with things available to them. Her father was a part-time Baptist preacher as well as a farmer, and church was an important part of her life.

After graduating from high school, Lois worked her way through Berry College in Rome, Georgia where she graduated with a degree in education and a minor in music. She became a schoolteacher in Trion, Georgia where she met and married her husband, Bob Stewart. They raised three children and have been happily married for over 50 years. They live in Opelika, Alabama. Lois is active in the Methodist church where she sings in the choir and substitutes as a Sunday school teacher. She is active in garden, study, and bridge clubs and enjoys gardening, traveling, writing poetry, and family activities.